Arthur M. Smith

A System of Subjective Political Economy

Arthur M. Smith

A System of Subjective Political Economy

ISBN/EAN: 9783337073855

Printed in Europe, USA, Canada, Australia, Japan

Cover: Foto ©Suzi / pixelio.de

More available books at **www.hansebooks.com**

A SYSTEM

OF

Subjective

POLITICAL ECONOMY.

BY

ARTHUR M. SMITH.

" So God created man in his own image, in the image of God created he him ; male and female created he them."—Gen. i. 27.

WILLIAMS AND NORGATE,
14, HENRIETTA STREET, COVENT GARDEN, LONDON;
AND 20, SOUTH FREDERICK STREET, EDINBURGH.
1883.

LONDON:
G. NORMAN AND SON, PRINTERS, HART STREET,
COVENT GARDEN.

CONTENTS.

BOOK I.

CHAPTER I. INTRODUCTORY 1

SEC. 1. The View.
    2. The Philosophy of it.

CHAPTER II. OF THE WORD WEALTH . . . 18

SEC. 1. Definition of the word essential.
    2. Reference to the arguments of others unavoidable.
    3. Two schools of Philosophy and two of Political Economy.
    4. Same method will refute the arguments of Idealists and Equality Economists.
    5. Mr. J. S. Mill on Excess of Supply refuted.
    6. The objective altruistic view of the above arguments.
    7. Reasons for introducing the above arguments.
    8. Wealth relates to substances or objects.
    9. Of the different sorts of ideas of substances.
    10. Wealth shown to be an idea of the secondary qualities of substance.
    11. Wealth notwithstanding an objective idea.
    12. It must, however, be treated subjectively.
    13. Peculiarity of idea as a psychological state is part cause.
    14. Therefore mind essential to objective view.
    15. Ability of man in reference to.
    16. Means herein direct sensation of satisfaction.

	PAGE
CHAPTER III. OF THE WORD VALUE	54

SEC. 1. Value other than intrinsic must be extrinsic.
    2. Of the origin and meaning of the word value.
    3. Of the subjective modes of extrinsic value.
    4. Of objective or intrinsic value.
    5. Of market value.
    6. Some general remarks.

BOOK II.

THE SUBJECTIVE VIEW OF WEALTH. CONSUMPTION.

CHAPTER I. OF THE OBJECTS ATTAINED BY THE CONSUMPTION OF COMMODITIES EGOISTICALLY CONSIDERED 69

SEC. 1. Some further explanation of the system.
    2. Civilization or progress in thought and action.
    3. Progress in thought, altruistic faculty.
    4. Ditto, philosophic.
    5. Of the progress in action.
    6. Of invention or the progress of thought in action.
    7. Of the treatment of others, altruistic action.
    8. Does wealth produce inequality or equality?
    9. Of wealth in relation to man's happiness.

CHAPTER II. OF THE OBJECTS ATTAINED BY THE CONSUMPTION OF COMMODITIES ALTRUISTICALLY CONSIDERED 101

SEC. 1. Of the cause which induces consumption.
    2. Theory of the subjective reproductivity of wealth, or the cause which increases consumption.
    3. Reproductivity varies inversely as necessity or utility.
    4. Theory of the differentiation of consumption.

PAGE

CHAPTER III. SOME GENERAL REMARKS ON THE
CONSUMPTION OF COMMODITIES . . . 119

SEC. 1. Of effective demand.
2. All effective demand is absolutely limited.
3. All our wants are satisfied.
4. Effective demand nevertheless constantly increasing.
5. The fact that we do not consume proves that we do not effectively demand.
6. Of the proof of effective demand.
7. The demand of the poor will not employ them.
8. Of the inverse ratio of demand and supply.

CHAPTER IV. OF THE MEANS BY WHICH WE ARE ENABLED TO CAUSE A CONSTANTLY INCREASING EFFECTIVE DEMAND 141

SEC. 1. Man's wants are never satisfied.
2. Of the increase and change of desire.
3. Protection considered subjectively.
4. Protection from the view of exchange.
5. Of the middle-man.

BOOK III.

THE OBJECTIVE VIEW OF WEALTH. PRODUCTION.

CHAPTER I. OF THE REQUISITES FOR PRODUCTION 159

SEC. 1. Explanatory.
2. Of the requisites for production.
3. Of the requisites for the continued increase of production.
4. Does nature contribute more to the efficacy of some employments than others?

CONTENTS.

PAGE

CHAPTER II. OF LABOUR 176

SEC. 1. Of the classification of labour.
2. Of subjective labour subjectively regarded.
3. Of objective labour objectively regarded.
4. Of objective labour subjectively regarded.
5. Of mental or bodily labour.
6. Theory of the differentiation of labour.
7. Of the effects upon labour of protection.
8. Of the limit of labour.

CHAPTER III. OF MATERIAL AGENTS . . . 207

SEC. 1. Of the different sorts of material agents.
2. Does material productiveness naturally produced favour production?
3. Does material productiveness mentally produced favour production?
4. Objectively the efficiency of material agents depends upon facility of conjunction.
5. Subjectively the efficiency of material agents depends upon difficulty of conjunction.
6. Some considerations concerning the opposition of the working classes to material agents.

CHAPTER IV. OF PROPERTY 228

SEC. 1. Of the origin of property.
2. Why it is permitted.
3. What purpose it serves.
4. How it serves its purpose.
5. Some considerations upon Communism, Socialism, etc.
6. Of the reasons for permitting private property in land.
7. Of the cause of rent.
8. Of the cause of the rise of rent.
9. Of peasant proprietors.
10. Of property in the improvements in material agents.

CHAPTER V. OF CAPITAL 265
  SEC. 1. What is capital?
    2. Of the production of capital.
    3. Of the limit to the creation of capital.
    4. Is capital saved?
    5. Of the altered circumstances of the production of capital.
    6. Fallacies respecting taxation.
    7. Of the capital of the country.
    8. Effects of defraying Government expenditure by loans.
    9. Is it better to raise the whole of the supplies within the year?
    10. Do wages come from capital?

BOOK IV.

THE OBJECTIVELY SUBJECTIVE VIEW OF WEALTH.
EXCHANGE 299
  SEC. 1. Preliminary remarks.
    2. Of money, the medium of exchange, theoretically considered.
    3. Ditto, practically considered.
    4. Of profit objectively considered.
    5. Of the value of money as the indicator of reproductive employment.
    6. Of the desirability of the coincidence in coin of extrinsic and intrinsic value.
    7. What does cost of production mean?
    8. Of international trade.
    9. Of the value of money and bimettalism.

PREFACE.

THREE things are generally noticed by readers of Political Economy as being wanting to complete the theory of the subject :—I. Reasons for the discrepancy between Theory and Practice. II. A Theory of Consumption; and III. A complete knowledge of the meaning of the words Wealth and Value. These three wants the author has endeavoured to supply. Those who think that the facts of simple everyday mercantile life are easily to be explained in generalities are very much mistaken. Nothing is so difficult to explain in generalities as that which is most obvious concretely. Liebnitz was only stating a general truth when he said, that to him all difficult things were easy and all easy things difficult.

To the philosopher and economist we would recommend a study of Archbishop Morton's famous fork, as containing the germs of the only means of refuting the economy of Mill and Adam Smith. Had the latter been true, the Archbishop's arguments would have been treated with the contempt which they had then deserved.

A SYSTEM

OF

SUBJECTIVE POLITICAL ECONOMY.

BOOK I.

CHAPTER I.

INTRODUCTORY.

1. *The view.*—The first questions which the sight of this book would suggest are, Why a system, and why a subjective one? and therefore we propose to answer these questions first.

In the first place, it is a phenomenon of mind that it warms to a system; very few treatises on any subject are much thought of by man unless a synthetic plan is to be found which will guide the reader's mind. The "Wealth of Nations" is a book without a plan that is sufficiently developed to be obvious, and has for that reason been objected to. Mr. J. S. Mill was one of the chief writers who strove to overcome the opposition to Political Economy, which was caused from its wandering about over the world of mind and matter, by pinning it down to a synthetic material system, and in consequence of the great power of Mr. Mill's system, his book has held its own as a treatise on the subject up to this time.

Many writers on Political Economy of great repute object to a system; and more thinkers of no repute at all object to an objective or material one for reasons sufficiently obvious.

We cannot help thinking that Mill himself saw how feeble was the basis of the system upon which he wrote—a system which endeavours to prove mind from matter; but at the same time we think he also saw how extremely hard it would be to render the system subjective, or to bring in mind as the dominator of matter. Mind is such a subtle power that to pay any regard to it would, he thought, lead to utter confusion, besides tending to upset the chief doctrines of his forerunner, Adam Smith.

Political Economy seems to us to be a dying science, for the more conclusive the arguments are which are brought forward by objective economists in support of their theories, the more utterly does man revolt, and reject them. The more conclusive the arguments in favour of Free Trade become, the more powerful is the protection man makes use of;

and why is it? But because you cannot prove mind from matter, more particularly when you use words as a cloak with which to beg the question.

In the first place, then, this book contains a system of Economy, because it would not be received without it, because those which are considered the best works on the subject are synthetic or systematic. They start with an idea — a fixed idea—of what they are going to discuss, and then proceed upon a pre-arranged plan. It is true the authors carefully tell you they don't know what they are talking about, but still they have a definite idea up to which they hope to lead the reader's mind, previously concealing the idea so as to prevent original dissent.

We, however, prefer to proceed upon the reverse plan. We explain precisely the meaning of the word wealth, and, moreover, explain it in such a way that the majority of readers, though unable to get out of the reasons for the explanation, will at once dissent from the view; but having raised opposition at first, we hope to be ultimately able to allay it. It is best to begin with a little opposition.

The best reasons to be found for constructing the system subjectively will be found by any reader in Mr. J. S. Mill's "Essay on the Definition and Method of Political Economy," where he shows what his view is, and why it is impossible to make it otherwise. To that essay we refer the reader. His reasons given there are so inconclusive as to justify the taking of an opposite course. Mr. Mill says mind and matter are so dissimilar that they cannot be treated together. If Mr. Mill is right, then Political Economy is nonsense, for no practical man disregards mind; in fact, it is mind that the practical man is always considering. Will some one be likely to want the article? is his view, never the view of Mill, which is, Here is an article, therefore it is a means of purchase, and saleable. In the second place, this system is a subjective one, for objective economy seems to us to have failed both in theory and practice, and in the latter more than the former.

Nothing will better illustrate the view of economy here taken in distinct opposition to Mr. J. S. Mill than a simple concrete explanation.

Let us take our opponent's view first.

Free Traders or objective economists, of whose views Mr. Mill is the greatest expositor, argue as follows:—Cotton shirting is wealth. Therefore it stands to reason that twice the quantity of cotton shirting is twice the quantity of wealth. The simplicity of this is beautiful, the results are numerous, and the conclusions to the vulgar mind erroneous. Mr. Mill, in support of this view, writes, at Book III, chapter 14, sec. 2, " Could we suddenly double the productive powers of the country, we should double the supply of commodities in every market; but we should by the same stroke double the purchasing power;" for, he says, commodities purchase commodities. To those who argue like ourselves, that is, subjectively, the falsity of this argument is obvious. Commodities undoubtedly do, for subjective reasons, purchase commodities, and twice the quantity of commodities is twice the purchasing power; but twice the producing power will produce twice the quantity of things but not of commodities, because it will not make our desire for the things produced twice as great, which would be essential to the things produced being a commodity.

Mill's argument is a mere endeavour to beg the question under the cloak of the word commodity.

The subjective economist says cotton shirtings are wealth; but twice the quantity of cotton shirting is not twice the quantity of wealth, because wealth means the effect upon man of the cotton shirtings, and by the limitation placed upon that effect by man so the wealth of cotton shirtings is limited.

This is the view which it is the object of this treatise to elucidate. It is a much more difficult view to comprehend than the former, which has simplicity as its recommendation. This view says in effect consumption is wealth. The objective view says production produces wealth.

It follows, though it may not perhaps seem at first sight to do so, that all objective economists are Free Traders, whereas all subjective economists are Protectionists, these views flowing naturally from their arguments. Fair Trade may be tersely described as an abortive attempt at the latter by means of the false arguments of the former. It is a jumble repulsive to true thought.

Two root ideas involve two systems of economy. The opposition of these root ideas involve two opposite principles of action. A third is hardly conceivable.

It must always be remembered that from this view the subject controls the object; that the mind of man makes matter to be wealth or not; and that therefore, although it is impossible to disregard the objective view, yet by coupling the subjective view with it the former is absorbed and controlled. That desire and wealth go hand in hand, and that the latter proceeds from the former. That wealth is wealth because we first knew ourselves to be without something which we have now obtained, and that the mere obtaining, without the perception of the not having, is not wealth.

With any theory of consumption such as that here given objective economy has no concern. It is, of course, a mental view of economy which, as Mill points out in the essay before referred to, is incompatible with his system. The reasons which urge the great majority to wear silk hats instead of the rush apology for a head covering which a savage uses, must be mental; for as regards utility the latter is by many regarded as preferable. Mind is in all things the motor power, and economy without a motor power is like a hydraulic engine without water.

The great object of objective economy is saving, or abstinence,—starvation that we may get a spinning-jenny; and we have no hesitation in saying that saving or abstinence is just the very way not to get it. To suppose Arkwright would have invented that machine without any necessity to do it is to falsify one of the best known of proverbs. No saying becomes a proverb unless true. We must, however, admit that economists, on their own showing, pervert the meaning of the word "save," as we shall notice elsewhere; still their writings certainly convey the above impression. These being the views of objective economists, any theory of consumption, such as this, which treats of the cause of it, and of the means of its increase, would be quite out of place in their works.

The effect of many economical proposals is perverted in the public mind by the use of the words ease and difficulty. Economically speaking, ease means less labour, and difficulty, more labour; that is to say, remunerative labour; and when the Free Traders therefore point to their system as being productive of ease, they mean nothing more nor less than that it is productive of less remunerative labour. Ease and difficulty therefore are words to be avoided as much as possible, but they naturally creep in in any discussion because of their comprehensiveness. This system, then, is the difficulty system—the system which considers how difficulty may be so used as to provide the labourers with more labour and the rich with more progress, the two chief objects in subjective economy, and the reasons for protection. Protection makes the obtaining of commodities more difficult. That is its object. First, to obviate the crushing effects on the poor of the division of labour; and second, to improve the rich by rendering the obtaining of those things which are commonly called superfluities more difficult, knowing, as we do know, that difficulty does not render attainment impossible.

He that gives his labour saves it, and he that saves his labour loses it.

Of all the discussed points of Political Economy, nothing shows better the difference between objective and subjective economy than the question of exchange. Professor Bonamy Price writes, on page 304 of the second edition of his "Practical Political Economy," "The first fact is that all trade is an exchange of equivalent values or services. This is the very essence of trade." Objectively this is true. A mess of pottage exchanges for a birthright in consequence of trade between brothers. Professor Price tells us this is equality; that the values or services are equivalent. Subjective economy tells you just the very reverse of this. It says inequality is the essence of all trade. A birthright and a mess of pottage are not equivalent, therefore they exchanged. If they were equivalent the owner of the mess of pottage would have seen no use in selling it.

There are three ways in which we may regard exchange, that is, three individual views from which we may regard it, and objective economists have chosen the one from which no practical man regards it, and which we humbly conceive fails to prove their point.

In the first place, there is the subjective ego-altruistic way of looking at it. A buys a hat from B for a sovereign. Let us take A's view of the transaction, the ego-altruistic view, the view of himself and the other person subjectively, that is, in relation to the effect of the hat and the sovereign on the two persons. A would say that so far as he is concerned, the exchange may be regarded as equal; he would, however, add to that argument the idea, that so far as the other man is concerned, the sovereign is plainly more valuable than the hat, for hats to a hatter are as coals to Newcastle—superabundant and valueless. Consequently, when equals are added to unequals, the sum must be unequal, and inequality from this point of view is of the essence of exchange.

In the second place, we may take the simple altruistic subjective view, the view of the effect of the sovereign and the hat upon parties other than those to the sale and purchase. Poll all the world who took no part in the exchange, and would they say that the value of the hat and the sovereign are equal? We think not. Any person other than the parties to exchange would argue that the inducement to exchange is getting more than you give, producing inequality—that but for the profit no sellers would be found.

Thirdly and lastly, there is the egoistic view of the matter, that is, the objective view. The view which comes not from individual egoism, but from the universal ego—the argument that the benefit of the hat to the purchaser is equal to the benefit conferred upon the vendor by those things which he buys with the sovereign. Now, with all respect to Professor Price and others, we say that this latter argument will only hold water upon one supposition, a supposition which is manifestly untrue in the great majority of cases, namely, that the effective demands of the hatter and his customer are equal. Upon no other supposition can equality in exchange be asserted, for if the effective demand of the hatter is less than that of his customer, then it stands to reason that the sovereign or his purchases will be more satisfactory to him than the hat to the purchaser.

So there is no possible view of the matter upon which Professor Price and others can justify an assertion upon which all their arguments rely and upon which alone the Free Trade dogma holds good. We have only to show that equality in exchange is false to show that Free Trade is a baseless and false theory.

We have, however, perhaps omitted one view of the case, the purely objective view, that is, the view that a sovereign, being one material object, has exchanged for a hat, another material object, and, therefore, there is equality. This view, however, is too absurd to discuss. There is also the question of equality in intrinsic values, but that is also put out of the question by considering the exchange of a sovereign, the highest intrinsic value, for a hat, a thing which has scarcely any.

It is useless to argue with people upon most economical questions, and more particularly to argue with those who call themselves Free Traders, for, having two different ideas of the subject, all the arguments must be opposed to one another. It is like two people sitting down to argue whether pigs are white or black, when one party means iron pigs and the other means the quadruped.

Objectively the Free Trade argument is unanswerable, is irresistible.

Subjectively it is the greatest imposition which ever hoaxed mankind. It begins by begging the question, and ends with a *non sequitur*. Its subjective atrocity, as an argument, is proof, one might almost say, of its objective truth.

We must apologize to the reader for our style of writing, which is generally considered abominable, but any question of science has not much concern with style. Ideas are in question, not the mode of expression; and, although a good mode of expression is desirable, the author feels unable to attain to it.

The ideas of the system are both simple and obvious, but their very simplicity is the reason of the difficulty of explanation. Political Economy always seeks to deal with the common facts of every day life, and that is just the reason of its being difficult to explain. Man acts like a philosopher who knows everything; he is unlike a philosopher, for he cannot generally give the true philosophical reason for his actions.

It is not too much to say that so long as economists persist in being objective, so long will they be completely unable to explain the meaning of the words wealth and value. Their idea of wealth paralizes their explanations. Here is the general idea of it which Mill and most economists hold, and how in reason can it be argued from?

Wealth means generally things capable of satisfying man's desires, but it is inessential to wealth that the things should be desired. In fact, the less we want anything the more that thing becomes wealth, as is shown in the above-mentioned argument of Mill's, that twice the productive power argues twice the quantity of wealth or commodities.

2. *The philosophy of it.*—While endeavouring to arrive conclusively at the meaning of the words wealth and value some ideas, which may be called philosophical, had to be considered and revolved, and a consideration of these ideas involves, to a certain extent, a philosophy. It is, however, with great deference that we put down these ideas, because we are, of all men, most ignorant concerning the progress, and systems of, philosophy.

The word "wealth" is an abstract general idea which the word "value" certainly is not. "Value" may, in fact generally does, relate to particulars, and its being said to be at times intrinsic, or within the concrete object, seems to deny at once the fact of its being abstract save from Hegel's view. Here, then, are two ideas dealing with a certain subject, which ideas are, as far as possible, asunder in any classification of ideas and yet seem inextricably mixed up. Surely something important, from a philosophical point of view, may be expected from a consideration of them.

We need not now go over the explanations contained in the two following chapters, but we must consider them as understood: the remarks we propose to make relating to the fundamental points upon which man's knowledge is based.

The basis, then, of human knowledge seems to us to be an innate, as well as an external, perception of otherness. As to the latter, the proof is clear and certain; we see two objects at once, and we perceive the separation between them which involves otherness. As to the former, the following explanation of Hegel's idea seem to point to the innate perception of otherness. "The idea, however, demonstrates itself as thought directly identical with itself, and this at the same time as the power to set itself over against itself in order to be for itself and in this other only to be by itself."

These seem to be the ideas which are contained in the Bible story of the tree of the knowledge of good and evil. That seems to be a concrete explanation of this perception of otherness. Adam and Eve were upon eating of the fruit of the tree, to see two sides to ideas which before had only one side, or to perceive an otherness consequent upon a severance of idea. Hegel's idea seems, so far as we can understand it from Professor Bowen's work on "Modern Philosophy," to be the same. All is first resolved into one; good and evil become one that is neither. Then this one, which is neither of its own force, evolves evil and, therefore, good. The perception of evil causes the knowledge of good.

Professor Bowen, on page 367 of the book above-mentioned, states the objection to Hegel's philosophy as follows:—"But it is reasoning in a circle first to prove A by B and then B by A; first to give me consciousness of self through paper, and then assurance of the paper through my consciousness of self." Now it seems to us that the basis of human knowledge is not consciousness of mind by matter or of matter by mind, but the innate and external perception of otherness.

Whatever we think of, by thinking of it, we are conscious of something other than what our thoughts are engaged upon, and that very fact, of which we are innately conscious, proves to us that the subject of thought is but half thought; proves that thought and its subject are not conterminous, and that our external assurance of matter arises not from our perception of it, but some one else's perception of it, and that the more clearly other minds than ours perceive anything the fuller becomes our assurance of that thing, and the more fully do we become conscious of matter not identical with mind.

The proof that thought and the subject of thought are not the same rests upon the severance of mind. The proof that thought and the subject of thought are the same rests upon the severance of matter.

The words "intrinsic value" seem to us pregnant also and full of meaning for having shown that the perception of another mind is that which severs mind and matter; "intrinsic value" may be said to show that the perception of another form of matter conjoins those two ideas, mind and matter, of whose separation we had previously had proof.

The above is an expansion, as it were, of the saying *vox populi vox Dei*, that is to say, that the most certain things and the greatest certainty in human knowledge is attained through others and not through self; and that, however true the reasoning of *Cogito ergo sum*, the greater truth would be *Cogito ergo alterum quid*. I am thinking of a thing, therefore I know that there is something other than that which I call the subject of my thoughts.

The investigation of the word "value" will, we think, be of great service to philosophers, for it seems to give the clue to a knowledge of the operation of the mind of man, and it is upon our explanation of it that the whole of this system of economy is based. The most amusing argument philosophically concerning "value" which we have seen is that of Mr. G. D. Macleod, who tries to show that "value," being extrinsic, must be in some other matter (that is intrinsic), and that, therefore, "intrinsic value" is an absurd and ridiculous expression, and that we might just as well talk about intrinsic distance. Any one surely must perceive that "value," being extrinsic, is in mind and not matter, and that Mill's idea of its being the ratio of exchange is false upon the face of it and so useless argumentatively.

The above considerations seem to point to the insufficiency of the arguments of philosophers who assert the indestructibility of matter an insufficiency which Mr. Spencer seems disposed to admit, for he says that the arguments generally brought forward prove the indestructibility of force. If the above considerations are of any value the proof of the indestructibility of matter lies in its severance. If I can perceive two forms of matter, then matter has been destroyed, for differentiation is destruction. That which is indestructible must surely be uniform, or what idea is supposed to be conveyed by in- destructible ? According to philosophers matter seems to be quantity and nothing else; because the quantity remains therefore it is said matter is indestructible ; surely this is bad argument.

We merely mention this just to show that, if the ideas here explained are correct concerning the word Value, we shall be able to find the true evidence upon which we may base any statement. That the true evidence will be obtained either from the existence or non-existence of some other form of mind or of some other form of matter and not from that in question.

CHAPTER II.

EXPLANATION OF MEANING ATTACHED TO THE WORD WEALTH.

1. *A definition of the word Wealth essential.*—It is before all things necessary in a treatise like the present to accurately define and fully explain the meaning which we attach to the word Wealth, for the simple reason that we propose to discuss it from a given point of view—from, in fact, a given explanation—and therefore it seems foolish to write a treatise and leave the reader to infer the meaning attached to that upon which our arguments are based. Any other course seems to be fraught with mischief to the reader, for no man can be expected to agree with another when the base and foundation of the arguments of each is different, and in cases where, as in Political Economy, the idea is hidden under a word to which people professedly attach different meanings, the definition and explanation of the matter prevents argument. If in dealing with any argument concerning our subject we explain it (the subject), then, and not till then, can an opponent say we are logically right ; and however logically right we may then be, it is of course open to our

opponent to say that he disagrees with our conclusions because he argues from a different basis.

He who studies Political Economy can only infer from the works on the subject the meaning which the different authors attach to the word wealth; and unless, therefore, he is a very careful student, he will probably not perceive the differences of meaning which are the cause of the diversities in the argumentation. Being desirous, therefore, of preventing future contention upon any other than acknowledged disagreement of ideas, we propose to discuss the matter from a given point of view, any other method of procedure being the cause of controversy and contention, which we desire to avoid, and productive of more wrangling than knowledge.

2. *Reference to the arguments of others unavoidable.*—Such being the proposed plan and scope of the work, it will seem at first sight that any notice of the works and of the arguments contained in the writings of others, who professedly write upon no given basis, is out of place, but inasmuch as any system of Political Economy is supposed to deal with the facts of life, to ignore others entirely would be to fail in our duty to the reader; for although our statements may be logically true, yet it seems our duty to show why upon our view of the matter the statements of others are false, that so the reader may not have the bare task imposed upon him of

considering the arguments *pro* and *con*, and so coming to a conclusion, but may be assisted in his considerations by a juxtaposition of the arguments. In addition to which it would seem to many readers as though we were afraid of grappling with the arguments of our opponents, for fear of being worsted in the discussion. At the same time we wish to avoid, as far as may be, anything like polemical controversy.

We wish to put the matter in such a way before the reader that he may go away convinced, or disagreeing with the basis of the argument and not the argument itself. It is very seldom the case, though of course it is so sometimes, that persons disagree about a logical argument: about the methods and steps taken to prove a conclusion; almost all men can, without any great mental operation, form a true conclusion from a given premiss, and generally any argument arises from our not having clear and distinct ideas of the things about which we are talking. Once let our idea be fixed and determinate, and argument ceases.

Keeping this object clearly in view, we propose to begin at the very beginning, to go back as far as we can in an investigation of the matter, that so we may prove our views fully, and let not our reader complain if we seem at first sight to have travelled far out of our domain into the higher regions of Philosophy.

3. *Two schools of Philosophy and two of Political Economy.* — Philosophers may be divided into the Idealistic and Materialistic schools : into those who, like Berkeley, suppose matter is but evidence of mind, or, like Locke, who regard mind and matter as different things.

There are also two schools of Political Economists: the schools of Theory and Practice of Free Trade and the Mercantile System, or, as we shall class them, the Equality and Excess of Supply schools.

These parallel diversities do not seem at first sight to have anything at all in common to at all resemble one another, and yet it will be found, upon a closer inspection, that although the form of idea differs, yet the idea itself is in both cases the same, and just as each writer takes up one idea or the other, so he follows out his idea to its logical conclusion.

The argument of Berkeley, for instance, is that matter cannot be proved or supposed to exist without mind, that the perception of matter is nothing else than proof of a mind perceiving it ; and similar in idea, though not in form, is Mill's much-lauded argument, that the fact that we go on adding to production proves that there is no lack of desire to consume, for it cannot be supposed that any one would continue to produce just for amusement.

The idea contained in the basis of both arguments is the same, namely, that matter is but a proof of mind ; but whereas Berkeley says so simply and in so many words, Mill says, a given form or description of matter is proof of a given form or phase of mind.

It is deducible from Locke's writings that he conceived matter as separate from mind, and similarly Sismondi and the believers in the Mercantile System believe that there are generally more commodities than people desire, that there is generally an excess of supply, and that consequently the fact that we go on adding to production is no proof, as Mill supposes, that we desire to consume, or to be more correct, that we give effect to our desire to consume; for we can only suppose J. S. Mill was alluding to effective demand when he wrote that chapter which deals with excess of supply. Effective demand being that with which alone Political Economy is supposed to deal. The idea of ineffective demand being allowed, even by Mill and his followers, to be outside the question.

The essential difference then between Philosophy and Political Economy is, that one regards mind simply as mind, while the other regards that outward expression of mind which is known as a desire or wish.

4. *The same method will refute both the Idealists and the Equality Economists.* — Such being the similarity of the two schools of thought, it will not seem very odd when we say that the

same view will expose both fallacies; for we may say at once, we consider both the arguments of the Idealists and the Equality Economists fallacious.

Let us take Bishop Berkeley, an idealist, first. At about a quarter of the way through the first dialogue between* Hylus and Philonous occurs this passage of arms :—

"PHIL. I think you granted before that no unperceiving being was capable of pleasure any more than of pain.

"HYL. I did.

"PHIL. And is not warmth, or a more gentle degree of heat than what causes uneasinesss, a pleasure?

"HYL. What then?

"PHIL. Consequently it cannot exist without the mind in an unperceiving substance or body.

"HYL. So it seems."

Further on Hylus says: "But after all can anything be more absurd than to say there is no heat in the fire?"

In the first place, let us regard what we will call the subjective altruistic argument, that is, the argument in this case from two persons and one fire. Suppose Hylus to feel the heat of the fire and not Philonous, then of course, if Berkeley is right, that the heat is in the person and not the fire, heat is and is not at the same time, which is absurd—no one

*See Errata on back

can suppose that only those things exist which one person perceives, and that each one's sensations are the only allowable evidence. Imagine a court of law allowing arguments like Berkeley's.

Imagine a case of petty larceny in which A gives evidence that he saw B steal the watch of C. It would here be open to the judge, if he argued like the bishop, to acquit B at once. He would say so far as this court is concerned the act of stealing did not exist, for I did not perceive it, and A is merely asserting that something existed which mind—my mind—did not perceive. It may be answered that A's mind in the above is as good as the judge's, and therefore the theft did exist because a mind perceived it, and so far Berkeley's argument is good. It shows, by regarding mind as every one's mind, that abstract altruistic truth is equivalent to falsehood, that that which no one can perceive cannot be affirmed true. But the fact that there is such a thing as abstract egoistic truth, or something perceived by one person and not by another, shows that that something perceived is without mind, for there is a mind not perceiving and yet the mind of a person, he who is told of the thing, who can, on good evidence, assert the existence of a thing. Therefore we say the heat is in the fire. When Hylus says to Philonous fire is hot, Philonous has good evidence of the existence of matter, *i.e.*, that which is on fire outside mind—that is, his mind.

But there is another very important fact to point out, and that is Berkeley's use of the words heat and warmth, the essential difference between which is, if one may so call it, the difference between subjective and objective sensation. We currently say, for instance, I feel warm; or, in other words, the sensation warmth is perceived by me; but we also say the fire is hot, which is the assertion of a property of the fire, and the reason of this seems to be that warmth is such a faint sensation that it may be, and possibly is, imperceptible to any one save the person feeling it, but heat is such a violent sensation that no one can deny it, and because no one can deny it we assert its objective existence. So that we may say the assertion of warmth is an egoistically true statement, the assertion that fire is hot is an altruistically true statement, and that which is altruistically true we may call egoistically abstract, that is, it is none the less true because not perceived by any particular individual, and as regards any particular person, abstract truth seems very conceivable.

5. *Mill on Excess of Supply refuted.*—At Book III, chapter 16, sec. 3 of his " Principles of Political Economy," Mill writes:—

" There may easily be a greater quantity of any particular commodity than is desired by those who have the ability to purchase, and it is abstractedly conceivable that this might be the case with all commodities. The error is in not perceiving that though all who had an equivalent to give might be fully provided with every consumable article which they desire, the fact that they go on adding to production proves that this is not actually the case."

Which, regarding the matter from the point of view of exchange, or as we have said above, altruistically, is no more than to assert that though A, who has an equivalent to give, might be fully provided with all the commodities he desires, yet the fact that he, A, goes on adding to production proves that B wants to consume. If each man produces for himself alone, and no exchange of goods is either permissible or takes place, then Mill's argument is perhaps true from this point of view (not, however, from the point of view with which we are about to deal). But as a matter of fact each man does not produce for himself and himself alone, and therefore in any case of sale and purchase, or of exchange, it is essential to true argument to show that what one man produces another desires to consume, or, if that is not proved, it proves nothing: in respect of cases where goods are bought and sold or exchanged, surely this is sufficiently obvious. If, however, a man produce something, it may prove that he has an ineffective demand, that is, that he wants something or he would not have produced anything; but in Political Economy, where we deal with effective demand, it is no use to say A produces unless at the same time you show that B desires to consume, or that A can in some way, whether by means of B or else how, make his demand effective. Consequently Mill's argument, just like Bishop Berkeley's, appears to us, from this point of view, to be nothing more than a *non sequitur*. It was essential to prove Mill's case to show that we are ready to give other material objects, of greater value, for the production in question.

Mill here gives us the same idea as Berkeley, for he says that the production of an object proves a desire to consume, which reduced to the simple form of Berkeley's statement would be, the production of the object proves effective desire in the mind of the person producing it. So that it seems the two ideas are substantially the same.

6. *The objective altruistic view of the above argument.*—It is generally conceded that time or the knowledge of time is the result of the perception of change in the objects presented to and affecting our senses. For instance, we know day from night by perceiving the disappearance of the sun and the appearance of the moon; this perception of change causes the idea of time. It becomes a metaphysical question, however, of great nicety, whether, assuming no objective change to take place, we could formulate the idea of time from mind as it at present exists.

Kant was of opinion that we could, and we agree with Kant that time is an *à priori*, but although we regard the mind as of infinite *à priori* power to produce ideas, yet the knowledge that ideas are not seems to prove that an *à posteriori* sensation is necessary to call such ideas to the perception of man. It may be said we could, for we should get that idea from the movement of one finger across the palm of the other hand, or by touching different parts of the body, but all this is producing exterior sensations and so conveying the idea. It is a question, however, too abstruse for discussion here; all we wish to point out is that Berkeley's argument that heat is nothing but a sensation in us, and cannot be said to be in the thing, seems to fail, because when the fire is taken away and a block of ice brought near in its place, we perceive the heat to be gone from us, we perceive at once a severance of matter from our mind. We have no reason to suppose that that matter has become ice, that we perceive still the same matter; and unless he can prove that, his argument that matter is mere evidence of a mind perceiving it fails. Had he shown that time was inconceivable, or, what is its equivalent, that a change of matter was inconceivable, he had proved his point, and when we say a change of matter, we suppose it will be admitted that matter is not one and indivisible, that the matter composing our penholder, for instance, is different matter from that composing some one else's penholder, consequently from the view of time or objective altruism we conceive Berkeley's argument false.

Similarly we consume different articles and not always one and the same article, consequently, to prove that there is no excess of supply of articles generally, Mill should have shown either that we only consumed one article of commerce, or that the transference of desire from one article to another until the former article was entirely consumed was impossible, or, what is equivalent, that the moment we ceased to use a thing it ceased to be a commodity or wealth, for if upon a cessation of user of one thing and the use thereupon of another thing the former still remains as wealth, then there is at once excess of supply, and from this we draw the conclusion that to prove the impossibility of excess of supply you must prove that all that is produced is consumed *in the same time,* for just as above the transference of desire or user is the equivalent (subjectively) of time or the perception of a change of object.

That the transference of desire or user from one article to another is the subjective equivalent of the idea time as objectively produced, may seem obscure to some readers. It is difficult to explain it, and the difficulty is caused by our regarding a phase of mind; and not mind simply for the phase of mind, is altruistically the quality of the object. That which is wanted is a commodity. But inasmuch as all human things, mind included, are subject to the influence of time, want or desire is subject to it, and so the change of the phase of mind, namely, desire, has precisely the same effect subjectively that the change of object has in producing the idea called time.

7. *Reasons for introducing the above arguments.*—With the majority of readers the above arguments may seem outside the subject of Political Economy and more metaphysical than useful, so it seems good that we should explain our object in introducing them.

The reason of their introduction is to show that there are two schools of thought in the science, to show that, according to the writer's view of the matter, whether subjective or objective, so is his view of its arguments and principles.

It is currently supposed that Political Economy is an objective science, that its object is solely to lay down principles concerning production, and that the idea of consumption, or a theory of it, is metaphysical and outside the domain of the science; that, in fact (as we have shown or endeavoured to show), an eternity of desire on the part of man must be assumed that so the theories of economy may be proved. And by eternity of desire we allude to such arguments as Mill's, concerning excess of supply, that the argument that we go on adding to production proves that we desire to consume, which is equivalent to saying that we have only to sit down and write a book to prove that people desire to read it.

This system must be regarded as a failure, for it can only be looked upon as begging the question, and such arguments are generally regarded as vain things vainly conceived. What has all along been wanted was a theory of consumption; some reasons which will enable us to guide and control the rash theories of the economists of production: and so this treatise has got the name of "Subjective Political Economy:" it is to treat of wealth, first from the view of consumption, and secondly from that of production.

In order to carry out this view it was necessary to show what the chief argument of the objective economists is, and why they err to give reasons for a variation in the method and treatment of the science.

Every reader of our previous works has cavilled at the meaning of the word "eternity" as applied to desire, and yet how else can the idea be expressed—the idea that we have only to create a thing and a desire for it in someone else is consequent upon its creation?

Readers of Canon Farrar's "Eternal Hope" will see that this is precisely his idea of the meaning properly to be attached to the word "eternal," that the word contains the idea of equality, and that, as he puts it, an eternity of punishment means not what it is currently supposed to mean,—unending punishment, which is inconceivable,—but punishment equal to or commensurate with the evil done, that the greater the evil the greater will be the punishment; and so here we use the words "eternity of desire" as meaning a desire equal to and commensurate with the thing produced. Inasmuch as production never ceases, then desire is called eternal or unceasing; surely as a meaning and in the use of words this is neither a misconception nor a misappropriation. What other word is available?

Again we wish to show why wealth is generally regarded by the public objectively, that is to say, as meaning the things which are called commodities and not as the sensation they produce in man, which is the same as the reason given above for our saying heat is in the fire and not in the person. The idea is so universal and altruistic as to become, in consequence, objective, but it is none the less originally a subjective idea, just as heat is shown to be by Bishop Berkeley. Again, a great amount of confusion seems to exist among the writers on the subject; very few of them seem to grasp the idea upon which all turns. As mentioned above, there seems to be among writers generally two root ideas upon the matter, and only two, and the object of the above remarks is to emphasize and explain the root ideas and the consequence of the divergence of the writers on the subject. The followers of Adam Smith and the leading writers on economy argue from matter to mind; their opponents argue from mind to matter. The first is the easy and simple plan, which, by begging the question, simplifies it; the latter seems so hard as to completely overcome the efforts of the writers, who write in a vague and undefined manner, and so fail to obtain the consideration they deserve. Moreover, as a certain amount of self-assertion is necessary to obtain a hearing in this world, so the vagueness of the writing of the latter destroys their self-assertiveness, and their tentative manner of writing causes the public to regard them as disbelievers in their own ideas.

With these preliminary remarks, which seem essential to putting into the readers' hands the means of grasping firmly the system and ideas of the writer, we proceed to consider, first, the idea itself.

8. *Wealth relates to substances or objects.* — It requires no argument to prove that goods, wares and merchandize are commonly called wealth, and that wealth is in the object just as heat is in the fire, but it is difficult to get people to admit that wealth is in man as well as in the object, that wealth

may be used subjectively, and that we may rightly say he who spends most is, because he spends, rich. It is the commonest expression possible among the uninstructed in Political Economy. So-and-so must be a rich man because he spends; that, in fact, spending is proof of wealth. It will seem, therefore, a difficult task to prove that the fact that merchandize is called wealth is no denial of the fact that spending is a proof of wealth; we hope to reconcile these seeming discrepancies, but, while we do so, the reader will find how hard it is to grasp the idea conveyed by the word wealth.

In McCulloch's edition of Adam Smith's "Wealth of Nations" he defines wealth as "things necessary, useful or agreeable to man, which, at the same time, possess an exchangeable value," and this is in some sort a very fair definition, and which at once shows the *crux* of the argument, namely, altruism : if a thing possesses an exchangeable value, then you are justified in saying the thing is wealth, and equally also you admit that some one else is necessary to a true conception of the idea, for two persons are the least number who can make an exchange, so that statements concerning wealth must be altruistic to be true.

It is then undeniable that things are wealth, and must be taken by every one to be admitted to be so, but very few persons seem to realize that their possessing an exchange value (an altruistic value) is our only justification really, for using the word in a sense different from its original meaning.

9. *Of the different sorts of ideas of substances.*— We feel we cannot do better than quote Locke on ideas of substances, for he puts his ideas better than most people, and we do not think they can be improved upon. At Book II, chap. xxiii, sec. 9, of his "Essay on the Human Understanding," he writes:— "Three sorts of ideas make our complex ones of substances. First, the ideas of the primary qualities of things which are discovered by our sense, and are in them, that is, the things, even when we perceive them not, such are the bulk, figure, number, situation and motion of the parts of bodies which are really in them, whether we take notice of them or no. Secondly, the sensible secondary qualities, which, depending on these, are nothing but the powers those substances have to produce ideas in us by our senses; which ideas are not in the things themselves otherwise than as anything is in its cause. Thirdly, the aptness we consider in any substance, to give or receive such alterations of primary qualities as that the substance so altered should produce in us different ideas from what it did before; these are called active and passive powers, all of which powers, as far as we have any notice or notion of them, terminate only in sensible simple ideas."

Some general remarks on the above passage seem

to be necessary in order that he may explain the word wealth.

And first with regard to what Locke calls the primary qualities of body. These ideas are egoistic ideas, founded upon altruistic evidence. We say a piece of metal is square because some one else has told us that that metal has the property or quality of squareness. We do not use the word square to convey the idea of square, until we have been told by other persons what the idea square is. That is, what makes it, square, an objective idea, or what Locke calls a primary quality of body. But in the case of the secondary qualities of body the process is reversed, and that is what makes these ideas subjective. For instance: I feel the pricking of a needle, consequently I call the sensation a pricking sensation, and others then can use the word. The public use of the idea depends upon the ego, whereas in objective ideas the public use of them depends upon the alter; and in consequence of this, Berkeley's argument about heat is a false one, for it is founded upon egoistic statements which are subjective, whereas the refutation relies upon altruistic statements, which would consequently be objective.

These remarks are here introduced in order to explain hereafter why the idea wealth, originally a subjective idea, has by use become objective, and why it is that the word seems to baffle investigation.

10. *Wealth shown to be an idea of the secondary quality of substance.*—The ideas which we have then of the primary qualities of body are, as Locke puts it, in the things themselves, even when we perceive them not, and are such as the bulk, figure, number, situation, and motion of the parts of bodies. Let the reader then ask himself whether his idea of wealth is of this kind. If you say corn is wealth, do you mean it is wealth because it is heavy or because of its shape, or for any other similar reason? One of these ideas of primary qualities, namely, situation, has a good deal to do with wealth. What is called wealth cannot be wealth if unattainable by man; but that can hardly be the idea expressed by wealth, for many things are attainable which are not wealth.

Some people regard wealth perhaps as the aggregate of commodities, making, in fact, the plural of the word commodity, and wealth, equivalent; but this will hardly hold good, for then you could not properly call a single thing, such as a chair, wealth; nor could you say, as is so often said, corn is wealth. It must be taken as conceded that wealth is not an idea of a primary quality of substance or body.

Let us then consider Locke's third division of ideas of substances, and, to do so, ask the question, is wealth an aptness to give or receive an alteration of a primary quality such that it will produce a new idea in us by our senses? do we, for instance, call iron wealth because it can be made into steel; or gold wealth, because it can be coined; or do we call money wealth because it will buy things for us? For none of these reasons can any one of these things be called wealth.

We have before called attention to the fact of the insufficiency of this definition, or rather explanation, of the third sort of ideas of substance, because it only imports an objective change, whereas we have ideas relating to substance which imply an aptness to give or receive an alteration of a secondary quality of substance that is a subjective change, and the word commodity is a very good instance of the third sort of idea of substance, and a commodity not only may but constantly does cease to be regarded as such, simply in consequence of a change of mind, which change is commonly called fashion.

Our third alternative has now been reached, and we have to ask our reader, is wealth an idea of the power any substances have to produce an idea in us by our senses? Do the things called wealth give us a sensation? and if so, what is it? The answer to the question may be read in every page of every work that any man has ever written on the science of Political Economy. Take a few titles from a few chief books, and you are answered. John Stuart Mill calls his work " Principles of Political Economy, with some of their applications to social philosophy." Professor Fawcett is, however, content with the words "Manual of Political Economy," which gives no clue to the answer. Francis Bowen, Alford Professor at Harvard, U.S., calls his work "Principles of Political Economy applied to the Condition, the Resources, and the Institution of the American People," and quotes on the same title-page a sentence of Mr. Laing's—"It is not a duke that has £50,000 a year, but that a thousand fathers of families have £50 a year, that is true national wealth and well-being." And last, but not least, Professor Hearn, of Melbourne, calls his book "Plutology; or the Theory of the Efforts to satisfy Human Wants."

The Book of Common Prayer has the sentence—"in all time of our wealth, in the hour of death, and in the day of judgment, Good Lord, deliver us." Now, then, we ask what is meant by wealth? Is there not one only answer possible, namely, the sensation of satisfaction or satisfied want? Does not Professor Hearn's title tell you that is what he means? and what else does the title of John Stuart Mill imply but this, that he is dealing with theories concerning objects in their applicability to man or the subject, that it is, in fact, not with the object, not simply with the commodity, but with its bearing on man, with its power to influence and to satisfy man's wants. Read what books on the subject you may, one answer, and one only, is forced upon us, that wealth means the sensation of satisfaction produced in man by a material object. Nothing else will explain it all; and granting this, although at first it may seem untrue, it will be found upon careful examination to explain all that is required, and to show that well-being and wealth are truly synonymous terms.

11. *But wealth is notwithstanding an objective idea.*—The above definition of wealth is entirely subjective, and it is universally objected to for that reason. The fact is that nothing is harder to understand than the question of subjectivity or objectivity of an idea, and even the great Locke himself found it so, for in the next paragraph to that quoted above, he writes, " For, to speak truly, yellowness is not actually in gold, but a power in gold to produce that idea in us by our senses," which is no more than to say that the idea gold is both subjective and objective, that gold is yellow, that yellow is a sensation in man, and that therefore, as Bishop Berkeley would have said, gold is in man, or gold is merely evidence of the mind perceiving it. The question is one of the most puzzling description, and there seems only one way to explain it satisfactorily, and that is the way we have pointed out above, namely, by inquiring whether the idea is based upon an altruistic or egoistic view.

Take the statement gold is yellow. Now, is the idea yellow a primary quality, an objective idea, or a secondary quality, a subjective idea? If you view it egoistically, then it makes the idea subjective; if you view it altruistically, then it becomes an objective idea. For instance, I perceive a quality in gold which I call yellow, and, as far as I am concerned, the yellowness is merely what I see; if I shut my eyes, gold is to me not yellow any longer. I have no evidence to assert yellowness or anything else; but if we argue altruistically, we should say the yellow is still in the gold, for some other mind has perceived the yellowness at the same time when, so far as I know, there is no colour at all in the gold, therefore yellow has become an objective idea.

But wealth being defined as above, as a sensation of satisfied desire, it apparently stands to reason that it cannot possibly be an objective idea, from the fact that the possession of a gold watch produces in me a sense of satisfaction, it does not follow that it will do so in any one else, and it cannot be asserted that it will. If it would undoubtedly do so, then wealth would be an objective idea like yellow; and this is really what economists like Mill struggle to make it. They try to make out that a gold watch, for instance, or, we will say, corn, can always produce a sensation of satisfaction, just as gold always produces the sensation called yellow, and so to make it an objective idea; but there is nothing in the world that will always produce a sense of satisfaction, therefore there is nothing that is always wealth.

The hidden secret about wealth as an objective

idea is the idea of exchange, which idea of course imports the altruism, which, as we have above-mentioned, causes the idea to be objective, for exchange is impossible without two people. Robinson Crusoe could not exchange his wealth, save from one pocket to another.

Many friends have objected to the use of the word, and are inclined to deny that altruism has anything to do with wealth. It is obvious that it cuts the the ground from under the theories of economists, but how exchange can be possible save between two persons passes any ones comprehension; and if exchange has anything to do with wealth, then wealth must be an objective idea, and so the sensation of satisfaction, which is intended by the word wealth, is imported into the article or object, for exchange cannot take place until the article can produce in some one, other than its possessor, the sensation of satisfaction.

12. *It must, however, be treated subjectively.—* What better reason can we give to prove this than has been given by Professor Bonamy Price? In his " Practical Political Economy," page 5 of the second edition, he writes :—" The Political Economy Club of London met in May, 1876, to celebrate the hundredth anniversary of the publication of ' The Wealth of Nations.' It is unhappily but too clear that a marked feeling of dissatisfaction with the

actual position of Political Economy pervaded the whole gathering. One speaker bewailed 'the difference of process by which Adam Smith collected his inferences, and that by which his followers or commentators have arrived at theirs.' The result was 'a vast number of fallacies which discredit the science, and a great deal of time wasted on what has been written. The full development of the principles of Adam Smith has been in some danger for some time past.'" The Professor's object in this and other sentences, was to show that because people like Mill will treat the matter as a science, and not confine themselves simply to practice and the investigation of facts, as Adam Smith did, they have lost the ear of the public: that by ceasing to regard the matter from an obvious objective view, and in travelling, like Professor Hearn, towards, though not attaining, a subjective view, they had ruined the position and prospects of the science. And so Professor Price has tried to become more and more objective, to turn the attention of the economists more to the realities and facts of life, and with what result? It seems to us that the result of the exclusively objective view has been to produce the very thing which the economists so much lament; that because they will not, possibly because they cannot, regard the matter subjectively, therefore people refuse to hear; because they will persist in arguing simply from matter to mind, and not from mind to matter, the public refuse to hear the voice of the charmer—charm he never so wisely.

Read the scoffs of Professor Ruskin and the writings of many another author, and you will see, if you are not blind, the reason why political economists are disgusted, and the public refuse to listen. All through Ruskin's remarks you see him struggling to infuse a little life into the subject, to show that wealth is, as he puts it, the possession of valiant things by the valiant; that it is the mind of man that makes wealth wealth, and not only so, but that wealth is useful as it influences man, and only in that view; and that to suppose that twice the quantity of coin is twice the quantity of wealth, is as silly a statement to make, as it is useless when made. This coin is wealth, not because it is called coin, but because it is possessed by a person who can use it, and because that user makes him a better man.

Again, however much it may be true, that because exchange has become of the essence of the idea wealth, therefore it is and must chiefly be regarded as an objective idea, yet it is none the less true that it has its egoistic and subjective side; that however difficult it may be to conceive Robinson Crusoe as a rich or poor man, yet it is conceivable, and therefore an idea of utility in discussion. In such passages, too, as that quoted above from the Prayer Book, where it is used to mean well-being, in fact just what we have given, the sensation of satisfaction, it conveys a somewhat higher and grander notion than the pettifogging meanings of economists, and such use shows conclusively that no idea is truly discussed till it is comprehensively discussed; that the attributing to a word of so comprehensive meaning such a poor and incomplete one, is about as likely to produce a conviction in the reader, as it would be to discuss gold from the point of view of yellowness, and then to suppose our discussion complete.

Wealth, then, must be discussed subjectively and objectively to be discussed at all satisfactorily, and must be regarded from an altruistic point of view, founded upon an egoistic one, for altruism is otherwise inconceivable; and supposing our discussion complete when our view is simply objective, is about equivalent to trying to found a complete science of psychology from an investigation of the stones in the buildings of a city.

13. *Peculiarity of idea as a psychological state is part cause.*—The idea of wealth as explained above has several strong and markedly distinct peculiarities in it, which distinguish it from most ordinary subjective ideas—such ideas, for instance, as heat, pleasure, pain, a stinging sensation, &c.; and it is to this peculiarity that a great deal of the difficulty of a right understanding of the word may be attributed.

If you think for a moment about it, you cannot

fail to perceive that a distinct psychological idea is produced by the not having or non-possession of any one of those things which are currently termed wealth, we mean the sensation called want. The word want expresses a clear and distinct idea of the being without. There is probably no idea in the whole language so intimately bound up in another idea, which yet upon the face of it appears to be so entirely repulsive and opposite to the idea in which it is bound up. What would possibly be more strange and incomprehensible than the idea white, for instance, were we necessarily compelled to import into it the idea black; or to take another instance, suppose it was necessary to our comprehension of the idea of heat, that we were compelled to imagine the greatest possible quantity of cold, could anything appear more strange and incomprehensible? and yet such a combination of opposites is absolutely essential to the idea of wealth. It is one of those startling paradoxes which puzzle poor human nature, and yet poor human nature, ignorant though it is, is not allowed by God to act wrongly; and the Mercantile System, so foolish to the wise, will be found upon a careful examination to have been founded upon, and been applicable to, a state of things only fairly comprehended by a thorough knowledge of this paradox. Disregard this paradox, and endeavour, by showing it to be absurd, to draw the minds of the public to that which is easily comprehensible and plainly obvious to the meanest, namely, the objective view of wealth, and however clear you may be to the ignorant, and however unanswerable your arguments may appear to the wise, yet the result can only be, it seems to us, just exactly what it has been; and what Professor Price so truly laments—that you have a science without a backbone, or an art of the lowest form; an art which, as long as it sticks to facts, is laughed at for being so obvious to all men, and a science which fails utterly in making one single true deduction.

The idea want, then, is essential to the meaning of the word wealth. Wealth means the having got, in consequence of the having been without. "In consequence of" these words show how all-important want is to the idea. The being with simply, is not wealth. We have always had the use and benefit of the air which surrounds us; we have, thank God, not yet known what is to be without air; and, as we hope to explain in the next chapter, this idea pervades that of value, as well as that of wealth. That value is the estimation of being with, in consequence of, or as the result of, being without. Therefore he who causes the being without, the severance between mind and matter, is he who causes wealth, not who produces, but who causes it.

The common idea of the production of wealth is utterly erroneous, and is a misapplication of words.

14. *Therefore mind essential to objective view.*—But there is still another psychological idea attached to the word wealth, namely, desire. The word want simply expresses the being without, the knowledge of a separation between mind and matter, it, however, by no means follows that because we are without therefore we desire, and if we do not desire in the first place, or if we do not give effect to that desire, which is the second stage, we have not wealth.

Desire is or may be called the positive form of want, which is the negative idea, and nothing is more intimately bound up in, and essential to, the understanding of the word value, than this transmission of the idea from a negative to a positive form. Every one knows, save economists, that value rises and falls, and it rises and falls from want to desire, or from desire to want. People are apt to import into the idea want, desire, that is to say, to assume that, because they have not got a thing, therefore they must desire to have it, but it does not by any means follow, and, moreover, is apt to confuse two ideas, which it is essential to clear thought to keep apart. The word want did not originally mean desire. We must ask our reader's indulgence for transcribing from John Locke again; no man deserves such high commendation for plain use of language and lucidity of expression; and knowing our utter failure in these two respects, we cannot adopt better means to impress this important idea upon the reader than by quoting one most valuable passage straight from the "Essay on the Human Understanding," Book 2, chap. 21, sec. 35 :—" The greatest positive good determines not the will, but uneasiness. It seems so established and settled a maxim that good, the greater good, determines the will, that I do not at all wonder that when I first published my thoughts on this subject, I took it for granted, and I imagine that by a great many I shall be thought more excusable for having then done so than that now I have ventured to recede from so received an opinion. But yet, upon a stricter inquiry, I am forced to conclude that good, the greater good, though apprehended and acknowledged to be so, does not determine the will until our desire, raised proportionably to it, makes us uneasy in the want of it. Convince a man never so much that plenty has advantages over poverty—make him see and own that the handsome conveniences of life are better than nasty penury—yet, as long as he is content with the latter and finds no uneasiness in it, he moves not, his will is never determined to any action that shall bring him out of it." To read the writings of economists, one would suppose John Locke had written in vain, for what do they say but that cheapness or ease of production, which is the same, will cause a greater effective desire to obtain. That the greatest positive good, or what they suppose to be

4

so, namely, getting all things with as little trouble as possible, determines the will, or, in their case, the effective demand, or makes man's desires to obtain greater. It seems rather as if Locke had written this and other similar passages just to forestall the free traders' arguments. The more you prove that protection causes difficulty of attainment or uneasiness, the more you show that its basis of argument is good, for, as Locke says, it is uneasiness or difficulty of attainment which determines the will, *i.e.*, the effective demand. Nothing can be plainer or more simple.

These ideas are so intimately bound up in the idea, wealth, that to attempt for one moment to dismiss them is to attempt the impossible; and not only is this the case, but the altruism which, as we have stated above, has become essential to the idea wealth, and so made it objective, is even from this view of matter essential too; for to carry out the idea of exchange, and to regard the matter from the objective view, it is necessary that some one else other than the possessor of the object should be a person who conceives in his mind the psychological idea of desire for the article or object which the former has. Consequently, whether you look at wealth from the subjective view, or whether you discuss it from the objective view, altruism is essential, and to state egoistic arguments concerning your propositions must be wrong.

15. *Man's ability necessary to complete idea.*—Perhaps this may seem rather a childish view of the idea, but there is in wealth an increasing or a decreasing propensity which is impossible, save as regarding it from a human view; it is man who cause that there shall be more or less wealth in any given country, although no doubt some countries are favoured by nature; but to suppose that those whom nature has by her bounty favoured are therefore most wealthy is to suppose a state of facts for which no warrant exists in the world.

Extremes of good and evil are to be deprecated, and for that reason we pray that we may receive God's guidance in all time of our wealth. It is an undeniable fact that some of those countries which are richest by nature are poorest by art, and the cause of this has been given above in Locke's words. Good determines not the will but uneasiness. He who feels his poverty or his ignorance will ultimately become either rich or wise. It is the sense of inferiority or imperfection which stirs us up to be doing, and it is from doing that our wealth proceeds.

In a little book we formerly wrote we gave this idea of man's power expression in what we can call the only true objective definition of wealth, namely, the result of our ability to combine A's wants with the means of satisfaction possessed by B, and that idea of ability seems both good in the definition and useful in the interpretation, and we simply desire to

4 *

call attention to it as part of what Kant would have called the manifold of the intuition, or one of the ideas which go to make up the complex idea which we call wealth.

16. *Wealth means here the direct sensation of satisfaction.*—We have above called attention to the fact that this treatise is written on a given meaning attached to the term wealth, and having now explained what is the idea with which we profess to treat, we must call attention to a limitation which, simply for the purpose of explanation, we put upon the idea.

When we say wealth, we mean the sensation of satisfied desire produced in man by a material object directly and not indirectly, therefore we do not call for this purpose capital, wealth.

Capital is naturally considered from the objective view to be wealth, and it is so, undoubtedly, that we do not wish to deny, but in order that it may be clearly understood and fully brought out in its many phases we denude wealth of that idea. Primarily, those things are wealth which satisfy our wants. Secondarily, those things are called wealth which enable us to satisfy our wants because they enable us to satisfy some one else's wants. The better opinion even with those who, as we consider, define capital wrongly, is that capital is composed only of those objects which in no sense satisfy the desire of a given individual. No man who possesses a spade or spinning-jenny finds his satisfaction or his happiness in neither the one nor the other, and however useful they may be they are not satisfying in themselves. It is, then, merely for the purposes of explaining our system that we start at once with the assertion that capital is not wealth, that the tools employed by a man at his work are not wealth.

In this question of the difference between wealth and capital you may perceive the objective altruism which we mentioned above in order to show the fallacy of Mill's argument about excess of supply. Capital is that which may be consumed in the production of other objects. Wealth is that which is consumed in the production of satisfaction. The words "is" and "may be," sound the keynote of the difference between time and eternity.

See Errata on back

CHAPTER III.

OF VALUE.

1. *Value other than intrinsic must be extrinsic.*— The idea of extrinsic value may seem at first sight to be new, but a few minutes thought may serve to convince anyone that it is not only not new, but only appears to sound so in consequence of its very obviousness having caused the disuse of the word extrinsic. All value save what is commonly called intrinsic value must be extrinsic, and the words intrinsic value seem to convey a very fairly distinct meaning to most persons.

It is as impossible to conceive a value which is neither in or out of any given thing as it is to conceive our being in two places at once, or to conceive infinitly such an idea is quite inconceivable, and no amount of discussion could possibly elucidate it.

Again, the word intrinsic as applied to value implies that there is an extrinsic value, for what could possibly be more absurd than to give such an epithet to a word as would, upon the supposition that there is no such thing as extrinsic value, be utterly useless? The fact that you call a certain kind of electricity positive proves that there is an electricity which is not positive. It may, however, possibly occur to a logician that what is not positive need not necessarily be negative; but such a method of argument, however scientific, is hardly practical.

The first thing to be done, then, with regard to value is to explain the meaning of extrinsic value, and to explain it in such a way as that the idea value may be supposed to be intrinsic as well as extrinsic.

The system of economical philosophy here given is one founded completely on the conception altruism, the conception of otherness, consequent upon a severance, an idea very difficult to keep in view at times, but one of great power in dealing with economical questions. In considering which we should always take the other view, the view cut off and distinct from the transaction which it is proposed to consider, we may call it the judicial view. The reader must conceive himself always as outside his object if he wish to thoroughly understand it, and must only take the intrinsic or interior view as subordinate to the exterior one.

2. *Of the origin and meaning of the word value.*—Most people will be willing to admit that the word value is an estimation of wealth, and when we say most people, we mean, of course, people who do not profess to know anything whatever of the theory or principles of political economy, for of course all economists and free traders who admit a logical

deduction deny that it means anything of the sort. This being, then, the currently vague idea concerning value, let us go back to our explanation of wealth.

We have shown that the word wealth means a sensation of satisfied want produced by a material object; we have also shown that two mental concepts are absolutely essential to a right understanding of the idea. First, want, or the being without the object; secondly, effective desire, or the being with it; and we pointed out that it was upon these negative and positive views of the concept or mental idea that the word value was based. What is the idea, then, which is common to both, or which is admitted by the former and not denied by the latter? There seems but one answer. Severance. The being without is our severance from the object. The effective desire, or the being with, is the severance overcome. Now, although these ideas seem mutually antagonistic, they are not so. for the fact that we have anything does not deny our not having had it.

Here, then, in a condensed form is the basis of the idea value. Value is a mental measure or estimation of a mental state, and by the circular argument therefore wealth is a mental state.

In order to explain what may seem perhaps abstruse and as incomprehensible as the word value, here is a simple explanation in a concrete form of the idea.

Suppose a man was at the top of a hill and was

anxious to get a piano which was at the bottom of the hill and was unable to get at it otherwise than by means of a rope passing from him to the piano, and by which he could draw the piano up hill. Then value would be represented by the strain upon the rope which would represent the force exerted by the man. Here you see the whole idea of value in its most simple form. There is, first, the severance between the man and the piano, that is, he has not got it at the top of the hill where he wanted it. Second, the effective desire to obtain represented by the conjunction or the tying together of the piano and the man by the rope; and, lastly, there is the strain or power exerted upon the rope in consequence of effective demand for the piano, which is the representative of value.

As we have elsewhere remarked, the word value is nothing more or less than the inversion of the idea comparison. Comparison is the result of an endeavour of the mind to conceive a difference or separation between those things which are either in fact or mentally conjoined, that is to say, when you compare one thing with another you are merely pointing out their differences when there is a supposed or actual resemblance, you cannot compare unless there is this resemblance, a fact so often and constantly brought before one that its significance is apt to be forgotten.

Value, on the other hand, is the result of an

endeavour of the mind to conceive the conjunction of mind and matter upon a separation between them either real or supposed. And it is just so well known that what is not wanted is valueless, as it is that comparison without similarity is impossible. Value, therefore, rises and falls in proportion to the suitability of the thing wanted to man's wants; and low value shows either that the thing is not wanted, or else that the difficulty of attaining it is small, in either of which cases there is less wealth. This, then, is what we understand by extrinsic value.

3. *Of the subjective modes of extrinsic value.*— Either one of the words subjective or extrinsic is, we admit, redundant; for if value is subjective then it must be extrinsic, and if it is extrinsic it must be subjective; but in matters which have been so disputed about we must ask our readers' pardon using such redundant words, as we desire above all things clearness, we want to explain our ideas in such a way as to compel thought in our direction.

The modes, as we shall call them, of extrinsic value are three—egoistic altruistic, and ego-altruistic; and first of egoistic value. By this we mean value which at first seems entirely opposed to our definition, namely, the value put by a person upon something which he possesses. Value in the case of heirlooms or relics of antiquity, or in such a case as that proposed by Professor Price, the value of a dead child's doll. Here at the very outset our idea seems contradicted, for the value is placed upon the article by the person who actually at the time possesses it, whereas we defined value as the result of desire to possess something we have not got. These cases of value, however, bring out most clearly the idea when righly understood, for our language shows the idea as plain as possible, for when a person is asked to value such articles the first answer which he gives in ninety-nine cases in a hundred would be, "I can't value it (the article) at all, for I would not part with it for anything," or "nothing will induce me to part with it." Here, then, is the very idea of severance put before the public at once as the basis of the idea value. And again, suppose the other person to answer, he would probably say, "But supposing you were compelled to part with it, what value would you put on it then?" The result of these sentences is to show that although the idea of severance the basis of the conception value may be actual or material, it may also be conceived mentally. Egoistic value is the result of the mind trying to conceive its separation from the thing. This mode of value, may, of course, be high or low, and depends upon our readiness to part with the article upon which we are endeavouring to put a value.

Altruistic value. This mode of value is what is commonly called market value; it is the result of the severance between a thing possessed by one man and desired by another, such is the value of a hat to a hatter, or of the corn to the corn merchant, and the intensity of the altruism is shown in the compulsory introduction of the other or another person from whatever view you take of it. The corn merchant says, "My corn is worth 40s a bushel," because he fancies someone else is without corn and will give that for it. That is as Locke would say: the other man's uneasiness has become so great as to compel him to give 40s or its equivalent in order to make his demand effective, and that is the value of the corn to the corn merchant. But look at it from the view of the purchaser; he says that is my estimation of my uneasiness in consequence of my want of possession of the corn, or what is equivalent in consequence of the possession of the corn by some one else in consequence of its altruistic possession. All market value is not, however, simply this, as we shall show later on.

Thirdly, we come to the paradox of ego-altruistic value, and to explain we must again recur to the meaning we placed upon the word wealth. We said wealth was the sensation of satisfied desire, and value is its estimation. Therefore, by ego-altruistic value we mean such an estimation of *my* sense of satisfaction as will satisfy *some one else;* and this is the highest and most all-beneficial mode of value, and it is the value of such articles as a person is determined to get at any cost and at any sacrifice. For instance, a man goes to an auction determined to buy a picture of Raphael's; he feels his severance from the picture so intensely that he will give almost anything to get it. Then, when he does that he benefits himself, or must be supposed to do so, for what a man gives for a thing is proof that his desire for the thing is at the least equal to his want or desire for its price or what he gives for it; and so he must be supposed to benefit himself, and at the same time he benefits the other person who either owned or produced the article, for that person cannot be supposed to have parted with the thing for less than its value in his estimation, and if he gets more than his lowest estimation, there is benefit profit or excess of supply, call it which you will.

4. *Of objective or intrinsic value.*—Of intrinsic value there is only one mode, as is obvious, and that is the altruistic mode — egoistic objective value cannot possibly be intrinsic—the value of any one thing must be in the man who values or the subject, and cannot possibly be in the object.

Intrinsic value is applied to any given article in respect of its capability of transmigration or transposition into any other article. For instance, to take the commonest known instance, namely, the sovereign. We all admit that a sovereign has intrinsic value, and by that we mean that it has a value objectively and altruistically : that is, in respect of the applicability of gold to some other object or purpose. The gold of the sovereign makes up the sovereign; it is the case, however, that gold can not only be made into sovereigns, but into brooches, rings, pins, studs, &c., and the intrinsic value of the sovereign is its value as gold, say as regards the manufacture of gold rings or gold brooches. Mind is here regarded as a unity; we all desire, or are supposed in this case to desire gold rings, and the mind, as it were, operates through gold rings at the sovereign.

But, conversely, matter is regarded here as separate, *i.e.*, as gold rings and sovereigns. It is, of course, impossible to abstract the mind from value altogether: mind is the basis of value, but in the case of intrinsic value it acts through another form of matter, and so upon the article to which intrinsic value is attached.

We said above that value which was neither extrinsic nor intrinsic was inconceivable. Will it seem strange, then, when we say that there is a value which is neither because it is both ? We allude to the market value of those things which are commonly called by economists, Capital—such things, for instance, as spinning and weaving machines. Such value is the most extraordinary of all values, because it is both subjectively and objectively altruistic. Suppose a man to sell a spinning machine, no one can say that the price was its intrinsic value, because the ordinary idea of intrinsic value would in this case be the value of the metal simply which composes the machine; still looked at from the point of view of intrinsic value as given above the value is certainly intrinsic, for the value of the spinning machine arises from its power to spin cotton; it is, however, not turned into cotton as the idea intrinsic seems to import, it is an active intrinsic value.

But it is also an extrinsic value, for it depends upon the desire of another person from the owner for the cotton spun; the owner of a weaving machine is not the person who makes it valuable, but the other people who want to use the goods woven from it; and, consequently, as there are two persons as well as two objects in creating the value, the value must be extrinsic. The essence of intrinsic value is that it regards mind as one, while it regards matter as doubled; but extrinsic value regards mind as two, and matter as under one form.

5. *Of market value.*—By market value we mean altruistic value, whether extrinsic or intrinsic. The idea altruism is essential to anything connected with a market, for a market implies exchange, and exchange two persons, and not only two persons but two objects; and this is

why economists have confounded value with what Professor Fawcett calls the equation at which commodities exchange, for it cannot be denied that any exchange of goods is dependent upon and expresses their market value, just as money expresses value in all cases. The goods exchange because their values are unequal, because they have not an equation of value, but the exchange rate is not the value but the result of it.

It is not sufficiently understood by economists that market value is altruistic always, and necessarily —that is, it depends not upon the market or the people who compose it, but upon the other people who don't compose it. The merchants in the market have very little power indeed upon the market at all. They have of course some power, but their power is limited and of the smallest extent, whereas the power of the people outside is great and almost unlimited. The consumer can ruin the producer if he choose; the producer has no power whatever, or none worth speaking of, over the consumer. For instance, the fashion changes and the producer's goods are *eo instanti* valueless; you cannot create consumption if ladies, for instance, give up wearing bonnets and crinolines, the producers of those articles are paralyzed; and although it may be said that in some cases, such as bread and meat, the producer has greater power: yet even here his power is very small, for cases have been known of populations giving up wheat and eating rice or potato, or giving up tea-drinking, as the Americans did. The producer's power is limited merely to making slight variations upon market price; and even in these cases it is well known that any merchant or trader seldom makes a price, but puts it upon the purchaser to do it. It is not the merchant, but the other person who is either the consumer or his representative, who in the majority of cases makes the price, just as it is he who gives the value.

Market value though generally, as we have said, extrinsic and altruistic—that is, dependent upon the other person or persons who are outside the market —may be intrinsic, and as a good instance or case in point, we may instance the sale of old building materials, as in the case of the Law Courts at Westminster: they were sold for their intrinsic market value, which is to say, the value to the other persons outside the auction room in respect of some other object which it was conceived by the bidder as desirable to build.

Market value, then, must be altruistic, but it may be objectively or subjectively so.

6. *Some general remarks.* — We have a few remarks to make upon this and the preceding chapter and, first, we would again call attention to what we said before concerning this book

and other treatises on the subject. Political Economy is here treated from a given view, from a point of view new and distinct from any other writer's view, and, in consequence, we have placed these two chapters first in order to explain both the reasons for, and the point of view from, which it is proposed to discuss the matter. Mr. J. S. Mill says that he disagrees with those who suppose the definition of words to be the basis of discussion; he thinks, therefore, that an explanation of value should not precede but be inserted in its proper division of his book, and we partly agree with this view, and should have placed the definitions elsewhere had not such extraordinary confusion reigned supreme in this part of the discussion.

Giving then the matter from a new point of view, it has been our object, by explanation, to show, first, what the point of view is and, second, the reasons why we look at the matter in this light.

The whole subject of economy requires to be completely rooted up and fresh planted. All other writers have written with fixed ideas, and Mill, especially, has very well illustrated those ideas; he was of opinion that nothing more could be said upon the subject of value after he had written; he considered, and we think rightly, his view as complete, but its very completeness only served to illustrate his errors. If a man were to write a treatise on dogs and were to say that it was necessary to the idea—dog—that it should have a tail more than a foot long, any one who wrote and said he had found a dog with a tail nine inches long would simply be travelling outside the subject. Similarly Mill, having written with a preconceived notion of value, to attempt to contradict his statements with fact is merely to place yourself outside the subject. Given the premisses, the only thing one can discuss concerning the matter is the logicality of the deductions. One is almost tempted to regret that Adam Smith ever published his "Wealth of Nations," for he had no stated premisses on which to write, and he assumed ones which were, we consider, simply erroneous, because one-sided.

He who first defines wealth and value in such a manner as to make the definitions coincide with the use of the vulgar tongue by the ignorant will be the first to write on economy with a true basis for argument, and is most likely to make his generalities coincident with the concrete arguments of a trading community, which is the primary object of Political Economy. It is useless to try and control the ideas of practical men with generalities deduced from incomplete ideas, though we must admit that Messrs. Cobden and Bright have, in a great measure, succeeded in inculcating false doctrine among their own generation : the generations to follow will as surely relapse, for more complete knowledge will show the errors of their arguments. To assert that a given mode of action will conduce to the wealth of the community, while, at the same time, you admit that you cannot tell what wealth is, seems to us verging on the absurd, and one can but stand and admire the fanaticism or intensity of idealistic grasp with which such utterly illogical statements are freely made, for no philosopher or scientific person would boldly come forward with such an illogical proposition.

But we do not wish to run off on polemical discussion, the object we have in view being scientific and philosophical.

BOOK II.

The Subjective View of Wealth—Consumption.

CHAPTER I.

THE OBJECT ATTAINED BY THE CONSUMPTION OF COMMODITIES EGOISTICALLY CONSIDERED.

1. *Some further explanation of the system.*—There will be many readers to whom the preceding explanation will seem both abstruse and philosophic and who will, consequently, pass rapidly over the first chapter in the hope of coming to something which may be easily understood of the people, and we hope, hereafter, to satisfy them on that point, but, before going any further, we think it as well just to explain the divisions and system of the work more clearly that so they may be able to regard the simpler portions from our

view and not from any preconceived notion of their own. This plan then may be broadly divided into the subjective and objective sides of the question, and each of those sides will be subdivided into the egoistic and altruistic views of those sides.

We pointed out that the rock on which Berkeley's system of philosophy and Mill's system of economy split, is the error of regarding mind as one, and, in order to avoid that, it is necessary to subdivide the divisions of subject and object into those portions which, by regarding the necessary division of mind, will be able to abstract principles which the egoistic arguments fail to perceive; and equally also, by regarding the separation of matter, we hope to evolve some new ideas which will have some bearing on the subject with which we have to deal.

It will be found, on inquiry, that many of the views taken on the subject are contradictory, and this, of course, cannot be avoided, for it would be absurd to suppose that all the arguments of one side are true and those of the other false; to suppose that either Protectionists or Free Traders argue falsely and without logic upon questions of importance. It is possible to view matters from more than one point; and in proportion to the comprehensiveness of your view so your conclusions will be true. The protectionist view is more comprehensive than the free trader's and so more true, but because more comprehensive, therefore, more indefinite, and less easy of comprehension. The protectionist strives to take in all and fails; the free trader takes in part and succeeds, therefore, in producing unwilling conviction.

Again, when we talk of considering the matter egoistically, we do not merely from the view of any one given person, but from the view of all people regarded as one merely in opposition to the view of people regarded as consisting of separate individuals, the interaction between whom is the most interesting and philosophic part of our system. Here the ego means the undivided; the alter means the division of persons: it is, if we may so say, the unity which we mean by the ego and not simply the individual; perhaps to some it may seem a perversion of words, but, although difficult, perhaps, to express, and not easy for some to comprehend as an abstraction, it will be found that in treating of the matter the egoistic view is the easiest and will, without much difficulty, be comprehended.

2. *Civilization, or the progress in thought and action.*—From the above remarks it will be seen that this is undoubtedly the most important view which we can take of Political Economy as a science—as the science of life. Hitherto wealth being regarded merely as objects no such view of the matter was either necessary or useful, if the only object of

economy is to answer the question, as put by the objective economist, how we can get the greatest number of pigs, whether of flesh or iron, disregarding either why or wherefore, then of course this view is outside the matter; but most people regard such a question as the above as not only unnecessary but absurd, for if we don't want pigs it is no use arguing about how we may best obtain them, and if we do want them the question of how many we want dominates the question of how to procure the greatest number, for if we only want ten it is useless to propose a plan for getting a thousand, therefore to any true system of economy the most important questions are why and wherefore, and the most valuable answer is contained in an exposition of the objects which we propose to ourselves when we try to obtain any commodity.

The object attained by satisfaction is not in the satisfaction. It cannot be supposed, even by the lowest order of mind, that any result attained by man's labour on earth is attained simply and solely for that individual man. Some persons may possibly take such a view, but this is taking a very contracted view of nature's laws. God did not waste the bounties of His providence on man merely for the gratification of the individual any more than He wastes the life of the individuals of animate and inanimate nature. It must at least be supposed that God has acted in a manner equal to that of any ordinary mortal, and we know that few persons in the universe live simply for themselves alone, and even when they try to do so their purposes are mostly thwarted and turned to some one else's benefit.

Stated broadly, it may be safely asserted that the object of the sensation of satisfaction is to produce civilization, or the progress of man in thought and action. That is the object of wealth. To suppose that England or America are better than other nations simply because they are more wealthy; that the wealth is in itself a good thing is to regard the matter from a point of view which is immaterial or valueless because material; wealth is to be desired, not because it is wealth, but because it causes civilization.

First in order comes a sense of uneasiness, then follows the getting of the thing which will obviate it, and last, the moral influence produced by the getting, but the last shall be first and the first last. The interior view is a change of mind, the exterior view is wealth. Looked at from inside, that which was uneasy has procured ease. Looked at from outside, that which was valueless has become a commodity. But however true this, the positivist view of the matter may be, it can hardly be called complete; it is possible, of course, merely to regard wealth in the light of Herbert Spencer's view, as inner and outer phases of the same change, but the inner phase of change is one of continuing power, whereas the outer phase of the change may cease at once, or, to put it in homely language, the making and procuring of a coat is the outer phase of the change of mind caused by colder weather, but there are still remaining two views undiscussed, the view of the effect of my getting the coat on some one else, and the view of the effect of some one else's coat on me. In the former case the change of mind which has taken place in me continues on in some one else; in the latter case we suppose the cessation of a change of mind in me, that is to say, I have ceased to want my coat because I saw some one else who had on a better one, and it is these two views which are the most important in Political Economy. First the effect of discontinuance of old desires, and second, the production of new ones, in a word, civilization. What then are the effects obtained by our ceasing, for instance, to want bows and arrows and taking to want guns of all sorts, or by our progress in the forms of satisfaction? They are twofold, the direct and the indirect.

3. *Of the progress in thought, the altruistic faculty.*—This is the first result which appears in man as a product of increasing wealth. Taking our point of view as the nation generally or egoistically, it will be found that wealth has caused the individuals to

regard their fellows from a more enlightened and humane point of view. Not only do we regard our fellow man from a more humane point of view, but we regard him as some one to be benefited. Wealth developes the other regarding faculty.

At first sight it may seem that we have travelled into the altruistic view of the question, but we are regarding here the faculty or power of mind as influenced by wealth, the development which is taking place in the mind of man, either the individual man or the race of men, and this other regarding faculty is a most important development, which it is just possible may become so powerful as to justify communism; but of this later on.

In patriarchal times, as we are all aware, each individual took a line by himself, he followed his own course, and with possibly one or two servants or slaves he roamed the deserts, and his hand was against every man's and every man's hand against him. Other persons were regarded in the light of the perpetrators of injury, and his first object on beholding any one was to regard him or her as an enemy to be overcome. But as time went on this aversion to others was toned down, communities came to be looked on as benefits, and a neighbour as an object to be squeezed, and one from whom a great deal might be obtained; still anything like competition was looked upon as an unmitigated evil, and although society forced people to be neighbours, and tried to persuade them of the benefits that would accrue from intercourse, yet still in the enactments concerning trade it was obvious that the injury was regarded as almost outweighing the benefit. Not till we come to modern times do we see that intercourse has come to be regarded as an unmitigated benefit, and people flock together finding that their doing so increases their wealth. Progress has been marked in the other regarding instinct, and people have found that more benefit accrues to them as a result of benefiting some one else than by the mere selfish attempts of their ancestors to grasp simply at the possessions of others without giving any return for them.

In the Middle Ages trading communities were the bond of union, the tie which bound society together, and the declamation of economists of the folly of our ancestors in binding these fetters on themselves is proof merely of their regarding the matter from a small and contracted point of view. These trading communities and cities mark a decided advance in civilization, they mark a period when men were beginning to appreciate the advantages of luxury, the increase of wealth, and when, in consequence of the great difficulty of getting the desired commodities in consequence of a rude state of society without, men banded themselves together to obtain the things they wanted. Later on the objects of these societies varied, and from being first started in order to facilitate the obtaining of the commodities desired, they ultimately became useful in preventing their excessive overproduction, in preventing the ruin which their too great success would be apt to cause.

The result of increasing wealth has been to cause us to regard others as people to be benefited and not injured; and although of course our object still is egoistic, is personal benefit, yet in these days of commerce, as we see in the commercial traveller, the producer produces and tries to get some one else to take his production, that so he may may get the equivalent, instead of following the practice of the Middle Ages of taking without giving in return. It must be confessed that our rich ancestors were little better than robbers, and that they generally were rich because they had injured some one, and not, as is the case now when men like George Stephenson become rich, because they have benefited some one else.

4. *The progress in philosophical thought.* — This is perhaps the most marked effect which wealth has produced in man's progress on earth, and is particularly noted by Mr. H. T. Buckle, in his "History of Civilization in England." He says, page 41, vol. i, edition of 1869, " Of all the results which are produced among a people by their climate, food, and soil, the accumulation of wealth is the

earliest and in many respects the most important. For although the progress of knowledge eventually accelerates the increase of wealth, it is nevertheless certain that in the first formation of society the wealth must accumulate before knowledge can begin. As long as every man is engaged in collecting the materials necessary for his own subsistence there will be neither leisure nor taste for higher pursuits; no science can possibly be created, and the utmost that can be effected will be an attempt to economize labour by the contrivance of such rude and imperfect instruments as even the most barbarous people are able to invent." Here we see realized by Mr. Buckle one of the most important direct mental effects of wealth,—the progress of scientific knowledge,—and although we shall have some remarks to make later on concerning applied science, yet it is necessary to take note of the fact that science is at first what some people foolishly call useless investigation, that it becomes afterwards useful in being applied; science always acts synthetically, generalization first, application afterwards. Art always reverses the process, and art precedes science, yet it is to science that it must turn in order to attain the greatest efficiency. This application of science to art is commonly called invention, and under that head we shall treat it afterwards.

It will be seen, in the above passage quoted by Mr. Buckle, that he uses the word wealth objectively, while we are using the word here subjectively; and it may occur to the reader that the increase in the number of our satisfactions has no tendency to cause a progress in science. Inasmuch as we are dealing with mental phenomena, the explanation must be sought for from them, and it will not, we think, seem, therefore, travelling out of the domain of economy when we say that the reason why increasing the number of satisfactions increases the progress in science is because the increase of the bodily satisfaction produces satiety, as we all know, and satiety in one form causes an uneasiness which moves us to seek satisfaction in another form; and satiety in the bodily satisfaction is the means of producing a progress in the mental ones.

It must not, however, be supposed that because this is so, therefore the richest people must be the most scientific; to generalize so would be utterly wrong, though it may be the case, taking nations as one body.

Man's capabilities in respect of bodily satisfactions vary; and what may be satiety to one man is poverty to another; but it will almost always be found that scientific men are those whose bodily satisfactions are easily procured, and in no man was this more conspicuous than in the late Michael Faraday. It will of course be said that in Mr. Faraday's case, for instance, ease was the cause of his knowledge; but this is a contracted view of the matter, and we think that as in the passage quoted above from Locke, the real cause was uneasiness, the result of simplicity of taste and an early sense of satiety. Those in whom bodily satisfaction of all the forms of desire is the most quickly procured will, or, we should say, may become the most scientific people; but unless the uneasiness, so often noted in great men, is to be found, to use Locke's words again, they move not.

The production of this sense of uneasiness in man is above all things to be desired as the first step in reform—the first beginning of knowledge. It is difficult to say how it is best produced; but an alternating method of contraction and expansion, or the production in the mind of a sense of ignorance of the subject, capped by a conviction of progress in knowledge, seems to us the best method of education. The perception of ignorance is the first step to knowledge.

5. *Of the progress in action.*—This is, of course, at once the most obvious result of wealth. Not only is there a progress of mind left in man as the record of his increasing wealth, but there is a progress in his actions in the results of his material labour. Having in the preceding section noted the fact that increasing wealth has caused increasing philosophical knowledge, the separated effect of matter upon mind, that is, in unapplied science or a knowledge

of nature as separate from those forms of matter in which we see the results of science, such as the steam engine and the locomotive. We now wish to call attention to the great peculiarity which most especially marks this epoch of the increase of wealth, namely, the application of that science to the results of labour.

The great contrast which exists between the productions of man, say under the civilization of Greece and Rome and under the present dispensation, is the contrast between feeling and thought, or between effective feeling and effective thought. There is a lower tone of feeling expressed in man's works of to-day, but a higher tone of thought than was the case formerly.

Strange and humiliating it is to find that with all our vaunted power to control and utilize the substances which nature has given us, we have yet to look to Greece and Rome for art treasures, which are unsurpassed by any modern creations of man. It would perhaps be going too far to say that for 1800 years art has made no progress, yet who is there now, or within modern times, that can produce works surpassing those of old time? But however conspicuously deficient we may be in progress in this form of civilization, that is, in what we call the pre-eminently artistic form, namely, the form that appeals to our tastes, to our feelings and sense of beauty, yet there has been a very marked progress in what are called the lower forms of art work in manufactures, navigation, means of transport, and general control over the spontaneous products of nature.

The result of antiquarian research has certainly been to show that although the ancients had beautiful manufactures, and were exquisite workmen, yet the moderns have far surpassed them in the variety and rapidity of their productions, the more particularly in the adaptability of means to the use and service of man; and it is this progress which is and is the result of our progress in wealth.

The result has no doubt been towards raising the tone and manners of society generally. The productions of labour have, by becoming more diffused in society, rendered man more civilized, more interested in benefiting himself without at the same time injuring his fellow-man. The great contrast between men of this time and of two thousand years ago is a contrast in the diffusion of the products of art. Less real destitution then existed, but more real poverty. And it is difficult to say what has been the cause of this progress, what it is which has caused mankind to devote himself to commerce and the increase thereby of means of satisfaction.

But although the highest form of art has been stationary while the lower forms have been progressive, civilization has concurrently produced a great increase in knowledge. Again, it is difficult to say whether knowledge has produced civilization or civilization knowledge, for the two go hand in hand so closely locked, that it almost tends to prevent a separation; but if we regard for a moment the fact that progress always comes from below and moves upward, whereas knowledge, meaning applied science, always acts in the reverse direction, we shall be led to the conclusion that civilization was the cause of the increase of knowledge, and that knowledge really acts as an incentive, an assistant, but not as the prime motive power in civilizing mankind.

The increase of knowledge marks this epoch of time more strongly than it has marked any other. Not only have scientists themselves made great strides, but the knowledge has been utilized and diffused, and applied with greater effect than it has ever been done before. This powerful application of knowledge and science to art marks a very important fact to the seeker after truth. We allude to the fact of the increasing difficulty of the struggle for existence. It marks a time when labour, that is, paying labour, is diminishing in proportion to the number of persons supported on the earth; and when in consequence people are driven to find the means of still further reducing the labour, for that is the source of most of our great fortunes now. When desire for labour has become an undoubted fact of life, at this very time more than at any other, labour is diminishing in proportion to its result in the production of things necessary, useful, or agreeable to man.

There never was a period of history when idleness was so universally decried as it is now, and when the question why this is so is asked it becomes increasingly difficult to answer, and more puzzling still in the methods of God's providence is the constant increase in the difficulty of finding a sphere of labour suited to the individual. It is a current remark that the tendency now is for the labour to accumulate in fewer and fewer hands, and a man has only to become eminent in his sphere for him to be at once overworked and rendered the mere slave of his fellows, to be reduced to a machine with no pleasure in life and no independent power of action.

This apparently evil effect of that which it has been the object of economists to applaud, is one to which more and more attention should be devoted. Life to be made happy and pleasant to man should be neither all beer and skittles nor all labour; and the continuously increasing volume of labour in one set of persons is apt to render others miserable to themselves and useless to their fellows. A counteracting tendency may, however, be noted which increases the injury to the worker, and that is caused by the fact that more must be produced to get the same reward, the compulsorily idle retaliate on the worker by compelling him to produce cheap, that is by making the reward for his labour smaller.

The idleness forced upon so many now is due to the increasing equality of fortune. The rich are poorer than the poor are richer, and as the differentiation of consumption is the prime motor power, idleness is the result of approaching equality.

Conceive a circle superimposed upon an isoscyles triangle, and you get a very good idea of society. The base of the triangle represents the poorer classes, the circle the middle classes, and the apex of the triangle the rich. Every expansion, then, of the circle cuts more off from the apex than it does from the base, and as the apex is the motor power the enlargement of the middle class is detrimental to the whole society unless at the same time there is an increasingly large upper class. If equality was possible society would cease under present conditions, exchange would be impossible, and stagnation, and civil death must result. Fortunately for England the objective wealth of the upper classes has almost kept pace with the middle, and the result has been a vast increase in subjective wealth. The difficulty, then, of finding a means of livelihood among the middle classes is due to the nearer approach of equality of fortune or consumption.

England is beginning to feel the effects of a pettifogging and stagnating system of saving such as is ruining France. Movement is life, and the happiest period of English history will probably be found in that of Elizabeth, when men freely got and as freely gave.

6. *Of Invention, or the progress of thought in action.*—The progress of modern times, then, has been a progress in ability to import thought into action, an ability which has found expression in the term invention.

Invention may be defined as the discovery of the applicability of a form of natural force to the results of labour. Speaking generally, it will be found that inventors are not as a rule practical men, or perhaps we should say men engaged in production of the given article, though they mostly are users of the article to which the invention is to be applied. It is also noteworthy that in many cases inventions have arisen from the first use by an individual of an article. Very often it occurs that a man making use for the first time of some article has his attention called to its failure in some prominent point of its utility, and so having his attention drawn to a deficiency, has applied his mind to find out a means of making that deficiency good.

There is, as Professor Hearn says, neither good nor utility in pronouncing a panegyric upon invention. It is one of the great and beneficial products of wealth, and were it not for inventors the earth would very soon be unable to support its inhabitants.

Wealth supplies us with the leisure to become inventors, and invention supplies us with a means of obtaining fresh commodities.

There is, however, no good in this world which has not a counteracting evil, and although the good done to man by invention is greater than the evil, yet an evil undoubtedly exists in consequence of the fact that every invention is an abstraction of labour, which latter is the source from which so many get the bare necessities of subsistence.

There are times when invention inflicts grievous injury on the poor more than corresponding to the benefit conferred upon the rich.

For instance, suppose the consumption of any given commodity to be as it must be fixed in amount for any given time, say a year, then the object of any inventor as regards the production of that commodity is to get rid of some of the labour by which it was produced, and in proportion as he is successful, so the capitalist benefits, for not only can the capitalist now sell cheaper, but by doing so he cuts down the profits of his compeers, who are consequently unable to pay their labourers so well, so that not only is the sum of the labour reduced, but the reward which it gets is reduced also. The cheapening of the commodity to the consumer, naturally tends to induce a greater consumption, but to suppose the consumer will not take advantage of the cheapness to save is to suppose one of the greatest marks of modern times non-existent.

The total result of all these forces, then, tends to fall on the labourers, for not only is there less remunerative work, but its reward is reduced at the very time when more is being produced, there is less labour and less reward given to it, and at times this become so marked as to cause trades' unions and combinations to obviate it.

Although, however, this is a necessary evil, the result of invention is a greater good, and therefore economists are apt to disregard the evil.

A history of inventions would be a summary of man's progress in action, consequent, as Mr. Buckle puts it, of the first beginnings of wealth.

7. *Of the treatment of others.*—This view of the result of wealth in influencing our actions is complimentary to the preceding section on the progress of altruistic thought, but it is as well to regard the matter not only from a mental or philosophic view, but as that view influences and guides our actions. Knowledge, the concomitant of wealth, produces toleration of the weaknesses and faults of others, and a more humane treatment of them results in consequence. It is not so long ago when in this country men were daily hung for offences for which at the present time the punishment was slight, and although we should not

on that account judge ancient laws and customs as either foolish or inhuman, but simply as the outcome of the weakness of the law, yet we may point to this progress as the result of wealth, as a result attained by its diffusion and a more enlightened knowledge, ability to enforce the ideas *meum* and *tuum*, which are the basis of modern society.

Wealth diffuses among society in all grades a better knowledge and appreciation of the laws of property. Laws which, however much revolutionists may rail and the semi-scientific scoff, are the basis and ground-plan upon which modern society exists, and the taking away of which, even if possible, requires from those who attempt it a knowledge probably greater than any man yet possesses of the instincts and desires of human nature.

Nowhere more than in trade and mercantile concerns is this altruistic action perceptible, and in these days of the telephone and telegraph the men of one place are producing for the consumption by men in another, and in consequence merchants are engaged in finding out the state of other men's desires at ever lengthening distances from home. It has long ceased to be for himself that man produces, and as a consequence of the ever-increasing separation between producers and consumers there has sprung up that large class of mercantile men who are all grouped together upon the vague denomination of the middle man whose business it is by bringing together those whom distance separates to squeeze a profit from each, small though it be. The days of direct trade have almost ceased, and the separation having become so powerfully felt has resulted in the production of co-operative and other societies, whose business it is if possible to ruin the middle man. The action has produced the reaction, and it will be hard to predict the result. Are we to see an ever-increasing quantity of the middle men, or is the mercantile world going to be turned into a vast co-operative store? The latter system, though tried, has failed more than it has succeeded. There are no doubt at this moment many successful co-operations in existence, but a still greater number have probably failed, and one cause may be found as the ultimate reason. The time has not arrived so long looked for by radical thinkers when there will be a unity of knowledge, a dead level of intellect in the world. As long as men differ in mental capacity so long will the clever seek to outstrip the foolish, pushing to make for themselves a front position among their fellows, and anything of that sort by which progress is secured is radically opposed to all radical thought. The result of all co-operative societies, just as a grandmotherly Government, is to reduce all men to the level of clerks and assistants to prevent as far as possible one man from lording it over another, to prevent inequality both of fortune and position. Not only in a co-operative society has no one man pre-eminence save such as is got by a temporary holding of the chairmanship of the directors, or the governing body under whatever title called, but there is no opportunity for any one to make a fortune otherwise than by fraud. The clerk who doles out the sugar and invests his small savings in the concern must remain a clerk to the end of his days, and that is just the object which radical thought considers so good. The production of equality, or the prevention of progress, for they are really interchangeable terms.

8. *Does wealth produce inequality or equality?*—This is a question which has been long and ably discussed by many writers, and particularly in Mr. George's recent work on "Progress and Poverty" has the former been assumed to be produced, and for that reason condemned. It cannot, however, be too strongly insisted on that inequality is the cause of progress. That progress is the result of man's endeavour to obviate an acknowledged inequality, and therefore the more fully equality is produced the more nearly do we move towards stagnation.

But is there really more equality or inequality? Mr. George tells us what, of course, each one may see for himself, that in rear of progress comes poverty, and that the more wealthy a nation becomes the more necessary are benevolent institutions. These facts are so obvious and so fully brought forward and urged by Mr. George that it is needless to dwell upon them. There is, however, another class of facts more obvious than the above, and therefore more ignored, the fact of the great production of equality by means of a middle class. As nations progress in wealth the higher and lower classes become separated by an ever-increasing gulf, but just as nature is said to abhor a vacuum, so society abhors and fills up this gulf with an ever-increasing class of persons who are neither poor nor rich, persons who, being seated in the mean, may be regarded really as the possessors of all the benefits increasing wealth procures to the nation. It is these persons who are ultimately becoming the greatest factors and the guides of the nation's destinies, and who, while absorbing all the benefit, are most spiteful to the upper and lower classes of society; they hate the rich because they are rich, and they despise the poor because they are unsuccessful. It is a state of things fraught with danger to society, for nothing tends to anarchy like equality; where all are equal none will obey; where all are right no one can do wrong. Perhaps there was never a writer who more thoroughly contradicts himself than Mr. George; he says, at page 336 of his "Progress and Poverty," speaking of Italy and the Roman Empire, "Exhaustive agriculture impoverished the soil, and wild beasts supplanted men until at length with a strength nurtured in equality the barbarians broke through, Rome perished, and of a civilization once so proud nothing was left but ruins," and this from an apostle of equality; one would suppose Mr. George wishes himself back among the barbarians who, thanks to their equality, overthrew a civilization they did not understand, or only understood sufficiently to jealously contemn. The barbarians perceived their inferiority and inequality, and, like the communists of modern days, they thought a violent remedy would cure all the evil, whereas it only resulted in killing. This book is written on the supposition that man desires to progress, that progress is the object or result at which wealth aims, and, consequently, the author is not one of those who condemns wholesale inequality because it is inequality. Inequality is a means to an end, and, therefore, so far as the end is obtained, is beneficial assuming the end a good one. The possession by one person of more means than another is not an evil at all, for it is that which causes the possessor of the smaller means to endeavour to obtain more.

No one can deplore more than we do the want and misery which one sees around us in any large and populous city, but however one may deplore it the means of obviating it are very difficult to find; in the first place every man who studies the question has a different idea as to the cause and, therefore, a different idea as to the needful remedy, and in most cases these views are taken up on a partial and inadequate view of the case; speaking, of course, generally, it will be found that the cause of all this evil is the doctrine of the survival of the fittest, or, viewed from the positive side, a want of progress in mind on the part of a certain proportion of the population equivalent to the average progress of the rest of the population. It is unavoidable that all are not equal and that therefore all cannot progress as fast and so some get left behind, but this can hardly be urged as a reason for stopping progress by the production of equality. The fittest will survive, and it is hard that they should be prevented from getting the results of their superior ability because others are unable to obtain equally good results.

There is no system of communism which would not end ultimately, if properly carried out, in man's extermination from the earth, for the object of each individual would be to do as little as possible. All the results of labour being doled out to each person in proportion to his need, his only object in life would be just exactly what all economists know it to be now, to get as much and to do as little as is possible. It may be argued that under a communism man's nature would change and he would take as little and do as much as possible, but we have at present no data upon which to found any such prediction, and inasmuch therefore as we must presume human nature to remain what it is at present, or with but a slight modification, the effect of every man trying to do as little as he could would end at any trying season in a bankruptcy and starvation, which would produce revolution and anarchy. It would, perhaps, be possible, by setting one half of the workers to watch the other half during their labour to compel a sufficiency to be produced, but seeing that under the present system more than half the people are engaged in production, we cannot help drawing the conclusion that a grinding tyranny would result, for the persons labouring would be insufficient to produce the necessary quantity of commodities for even a moderate state of wealth and prosperity.

Under the present systems of Economy every man tries to do as little and to get as much as he can, but the result of competition as applied is such as to compel each man to vie with his neighbour in producing either a greater quantity or a better quality, and that is the means by which at the present time production exceeds consumption.

Take away the competition and let the other force operate and production is destroyed, and the result of man's labour abstracted, saving becomes next door to impossible, and the only saving becomes hoarding.

As we have pointed out above, the great good obtained under the present system is the progress in altruistic thought and action; it is now chiefly by benefiting some one else that a great fortune becomes a possibility, and the benefit given to the community returns with fourfold effect on the giver.

9. *Of wealth in relation to man's happiness.*—It is, of course, the current supposition that wealth is happiness, or that with wealth happiness is increased, and regarding wealth subjectively it would seem a necessary corollary, for the satisfaction of our desires is surely all we want, and if they are satisfied we must be happy; yet as Shakespeare says, happiness is best attained by being seated in the mean—that is, by not getting all our desires satisfied—and why is this? It is strange, but true, that the more we are satisfied the more uneasy we get; always restless, ever-moving man no sooner gets what he wants than he wants something more.

Our means of satisfaction are always overtaking our wants, but at the same time it very seldom happens that we are satisfied. Now in this matter of satisfactions there is a limit, but uneasiness is unlimited, not we mean simply as regards its increase but as regards our ability to satisfy it; and so it happens that when men have satisfied their wants they ultimately become uneasy, with a craving for they know not what, which they are consequently unable to satisfy, and as Dr. Watts said, then

"Satan finds some mischief still for idle hands to do."

If a man is seated in the mean his uneasiness is capable of being satisfied by means which he is perhaps able to obtain with some little trouble, and it depends upon the quantity or force of uneasiness whether he will take the trouble, whereas as he gets on in life his wants get harder to satisfy in consequence of their increasing indefiniteness, and it is this which causes the trouble. As long as a man's desires are definite he can aim directly at obviating the uneasiness that causes them, but there comes a time of increasing restlessness consequent upon increasing indefiniteness in desire, and then man cannot satisfy his wants.

Not only, however, is subjective wealth regarded as happiness or productive of it, but it cannot be denied that labour or the means of obtaining satisfaction is also productive of happiness; and it is this which seems to puzzle the objective economist, for the labour given in obtaining wealth is an element in the happiness; not only is the satisfaction happiness, but the means of procuring that satisfaction is happiness, and therefore when the objective economist tells us that because men strive to satisfy their wants with the least labour, therefore the least labour is the most beneficial, they are propounding a most erroneous conclusion.

The fact that men take the easiest way is no proof

whatever that they think most happiness is thereby attained, and if men were separated it would be found that what we say is true, that labour is an ingredient in happiness, but because men compete and judge therefrom, therefore they are apt to suppose the least labour the most beneficial, for the least labour gets most in objects in the same time; but the objects simply are not wealth, and therefore the possession of most objects is not necessarily the greatest wealth.

Taking the price of articles, for instance, as their monetary estimation as wealth, or the power they have to produce it, it will be found that the greater portion of the price goes to remunerate labour, and not in capital and rent, and this proves that the greater labour is, the greater wealth, objectively considered; for the objective remuneration is the smaller of the two portions. Regarding wealth as the satisfaction of the buyer, or subjectively, it will be obvious that the price he paid represents his happiness in possession or he would not have paid it; while regarding wealth objectively, it is found that the majority of the return represents the happiness of the producers. So that whatever view you take of wealth, the matter should be considered in relation to happiness, or the greatest good of the greatest number; therefore the argument that the least labour is the greatest happiness is untrue, and, to say the least of it, erroneous.

Of course if people choose to regard things as wealth, then they are quite right in disregarding all the questions we have brought forward as to man's happiness or his wants, or anything else. If we are only to argue concerning which plan produces most steam engines, assuming that an unlimited number are wanted and will therefore be produced, it is childish to discuss any question of economies. To argue with people who always beg the question from their opponent's view, is to waste words, because you must always be wrong; our only reason for writing is because we consider such reasoning, however true, useless.

It should, from the subjective view of wealth, be considered—1, how happiness is concerned with wealth; 2, whether all and what productions are commodities; and 3, whether more labour is beneficial in producing happiness or not. This is, of course, taking a very wide scope; but the wider the scope the better, because the more clearly we must perceive the truth; small and contracted views always lead to erroneous conclusions, and in no case is this more obvious than in the Free Trade theory.

When we consider, then, the enormous bearing that wealth must have on the happiness of man, it can hardly be out of or foolish to discuss its bearing upon that happiness, and in calling attention to Shakespeare's remark and the reasons of its truth,

7 *

namely, the increasing indefiniteness of man's desires as he increases in ability to satisfy them, we do not think we have travelled out of the domain of economy into ethics or anything else, and in calling attention to the fact that economy in our satisfactions is productive of happiness, and that therefore economy in production is not always good, we are merely endeavouring to assist our reader to the reasons which will enable him to take a truer and more enlarged view of the factors with which, to be a true economist, he must deal. That economy of production is not all-important, nor so beneficial as an increasing though regulated consumption.

CHAPTER II.

THE OBJECTS ATTAINED BY THE CONSUMPTION OF COMMODITIES ALTRUISTICALLY CONSIDERED.

1. *Of the cause which induces consumption.*—It has often been remarked of drunkenness that it is merely the result of a craving for the immaterial, that the feelings which induce a man to get drunk are those which seem to bring him nearer to the elysian fields, and is it not the case with wealth also? Can any one assign another reason why we should generally prefer those things, the utility of which gets less with their costliness; why, for instance, do we prefer a gold watch to a silver one, or a jewelled cane to a sixpenny vine stick? In point of mere utility the former is in most cases inferior to the latter, but still the one is preferred for a seemingly inexplicable reason.

There are no doubt many instances in which the preference is given in consequence of mere utility; but even in these cases, when we consider Locke's words concerning uneasiness, we shall see that, after all, there is a sense of the immaterial present which causes us to move, the immateriality is subjective instead of objective. When Locke says, convince a man never so much that the handsome conveniences of life are better than nasty penury, yet unless he is made uneasy his will moves not, he shows us; that mere immateriality, if we may be allowed to call it so, in the thing is no use in regard of its power to cause a man's will to move it is necessary that you make him uneasy or give him a sense of his want of immateriality, a feeling that he is without a something which, had he got, would bring him nearer to the ideal happiness at which all, save the stoics and the atheists, aim. It seems therefore to us that it is this sense of a world beyond the grave, of a time when uneasiness will be no more, that causes man to labour and to wait for a happiness which is a precursor of the better land for which he hopes.

It is very hard indeed to say why, for instance, fashions change, or what good any one procures by the change save the trades affected by it. The benefits that accrue to the traders are obvious, for it enables them to get higher profits on the ground of uncertainty, than which nothing more fully stimulates business, as may be instanced in the gold mines, for directly gold-mining becomes a certain source of profit the profits procured by it as a business diminish. Life is stimulated by gambling, whether at a roulette table on the stock exchange, or in the more stable walks of trade; and although it is considered so reprehensible, yet it has its beneficial effects, though they are outweighed by the evil ones.

The common explanation of the cause of consumption of course is convenience. So-and-so is said to be much better. A large house is preferable to a small one, a private carriage to the compulsory use of a public one; but after all the question forces itself upon us, why is it so? Supposing two houses of equal size. Why do we pay higher for one in a fashionable neighbourhood in preference to one more conveniently situate? Why do we wear gold watches when silver ones are cheaper and stronger and just as useful; is it not for the reason given above, because of a fancied more than a real benefit; is not there a sort of satisfaction in spending even though the spending be objectless or approximately so?

However much the objective economist may prefer utility, human nature will not agree with him. Utility is undoubtedly an object, but by no means the greater or more powerful motor power in causing the consumption of commodities, which is wealth, pleasure and happiness. Bodily satisfactions are immaterial, and the causes which induce a higher style of living—better food, clothes and houses—seem necessarily to partake of the immateriality of the body, to which they stand related.

2. *Theory of reproductivity, or the cause which increases consumption.*—No doubt many of our remarks will be considered common-place and obvious, and this

proposition not the least obvious of them. Wealth and happiness are procured more in society than apart; and just as the meeting of friends is a cause of happiness, so the meeting of consumers is a cause of consumption.

In no case is consumption so slow and progress so small as among isolated communities, and Robinson Crusoe is an instance in point, though perhaps not a good one, because overdone and exaggerated. The country districts of Russia may be opposed to Paris or London to see the effect of aggregation upon wealth, not only in increasing consumption but in increasing production. It will always be found that at any great commercial centre the consumption is increased in volume and rapidity, and the more it is increased the more man benefits; and therefore, as Professor Hearn has pointed out on page 20 of his "Plutology," the ascetic doctrine in relation to man's wants is both erroneous and absurd. It is consumption at which we aim, which is wealth, and therefore to keep down consumption is to abolish wealth, civilization and progress. The increasing consumption consequent upon the aggregation of population is just that which causes human progress—which stimulates man to try and satisfy his wants and to increase their number, that both by satisfying and by procuring their satisfaction he may get wealth, and improve his mental and bodily condition.

Professor Hearn also remarks, on page 22 of his "Plutology":—The question is not whether a given object be conducive to our well-being, but simply whether it be enjoyable." This is certainly, we think, the great object of all economy, if wants are productive of enjoyment by satisfaction, that is all a political economist need to inquire; and the fact that by aggregation enjoyment is increased, and as is shown by a consideration of the states of different countries, that wants are increased too, then that is a fact worth consideration in any treatise on economy.

This increase or stimulation of our wants is the altruistic action which is so deserving of consideration. It is, as people have remarked upon the Lord Mayor's Show, not the effect of the procession upon the Lord Mayor, but upon the humble apprentice, that constitutes the good effects of that pageant; and similarly in Political Economy. It is not merely the satisfaction which one person procures by labouring to obtain any given commodity, but the effect of the gratification upon his neighbour which is so all-important in the science. Individual benefits are of course to be considered, but in relation to the science of Politics or Political Economy, the otherness of the benefit is the greater consideration.

Politics may be roughly defined as the science of otherness, the science which treats of human actions from the point of view of the others who are benefited and injured thereby. Politically, theft is a great evil, and why? The person who steals gets a benefit which compensates for the injury he must be supposed to produce on the person whose goods he takes; therefore, if one is benefited equally to the injury of the other, where is the evil? The evil is in the effect produced by the action upon others. The science of politics virtually is founded upon the schoolboy's argument—those that ask, shan't have. When the injured person goes to the State and asks for redress, the State, in granting or refusing, should not consider the person asking otherwise than from a secondary point of view. It is the primary object to find out if the redress will benefit or injure, not the petitioner, but the other persons in the community; and it should found its decision upon the regard it pays to them and not to the petitioner.

As then economy is to be political, it is to be the science of economy from the other person's point of view; and to the consumer who asks for Free Trade, the State replies with the producer who wants protection.

Were the ascetic economists to keep their objects fully and always in view, and to be consistent, their great object should be to isolate man and so retard consumption, to place individuals in such a position that the gratification procured by A might not influence B in causing him to desire a like gratification; and this consideration is quite sufficient to show the absurdity of a system which hopes to stimulate wealth by keeping down consumption, which argues that the less we want, the more we shall labour not to satisfy our wants, but for the amusement of producing objects which, when produced, must be useless.

3. *Reproductivity varies inversely as necessity or utility.*—This statement may at first sight seem ridiculous, at a second sight be productive of opposition in the reader's mind, but at the same time we think it to be both true and important as showing the reason why those economists who believe in the ascetic doctrine act wisely, while those who, like Professor Hearn and ourselves, believe that as consumption is the object with which we labour, and as consumption is or must be acknowledged from our view to be a good, therefore, he who aims at its stimulation works for the benefit of his kind, though possibly not for his own benefit; that the spendthrift benefits others, though not himself, and therefore from the politician's view is conferring a benefit upon society.

In the first place, some explanation is essential of the word necessity—for unless the reader understands what the author means by his words, he cannot understand the meaning of the proposition.

Many meanings may possibly be given to the word necessary; but by it we mean that secondary quality in a thing which renders its abstraction extremely painful.

To further explain. There are no wants save that for food, which are absolutely necessary for man's existence on earth. The majority of the things we want are merely superfluities as regards our power of existence; but in proportion as a man, after rising in position in society, attains to a certain fixed level, then those wants, the satisfaction of which was before regarded by him as of no great importance, or by no means necessary, becomes very essential to his happiness, and the abstraction of those satisfactions causes him a great deal of pain and annoyance, which he would not have felt had he still remained at the same level in society from which he set out. So that the degree of necessity rises in society, and the necessaries of one man are not the necessaries of another—a fact so obvious as to have received legal recognition.

But now take the question of reproductivity. We have said that the cause of consumption was a craving after the immaterial, and this leads us to the conclusion that the more useless or unnecessary a thing is the more it represents the power which causes consumption, namely, immateriality. Take, for instance, the desire for gold and jewels, neither of which are of any great utility. There are, of course, a few things for which gold is of utility; but compared to iron, lead, or copper, its utility is of the smallest. Who would, even if he could, make a steam engine of gold, if gold were cheaper than iron; or who would build ships of it, or make it into fireirons? No one. So that its utility must be regarded as virtually *nil*. There is, however, in gold just this immateriality which, combined with its scarcity, render it much desired by man, so that the possession of it will cause a great deal more desire in other persons than iron, tin, or copper.

In consequence then of this craving after the immaterial, the more a thing becomes of use materially the less it is productive of desire; the more you render a thing of use, the less regard is paid to it by man, who is always craving for more.

But utility and necessity go hand in hand. It is necessity which renders a thing useful. A certain state of society has rendered rapid travelling necessary, and therefore useful. If it became unnecessary to travel, then we should regard it as a mere superfluity, and not therefore useful. Things pass into the domain of use, and are forgotten almost by consumers until they are abstracted, and the slightest abstraction causes uneasiness, and uneasiness effective demand.

Inasmuch, then, as the number of things consumed is limited, and as the immateriality represented by them is the cause of their being reproductive of desire, so the more necessary or material those things become to man, the more their power of reproducing desire ceases.

We have stated that the number of things consumed is limited, and we must ask the reader to take that for granted at present; later on we propose to justify a statement, which many deny by implication, if not in reality.

The above is a most important biologic law transferred into Political Economy, and it will therefore, perhaps, not seem much out of place if we just refer to others whose writings bear out biologically a law recognized by the public in economics.

Mr. Doubleday was the first, or one of the first, we believe, to point out this law of inverse reproductivity, and of course got duly laughed at for his pains by many people. On page 5 of the third edition of his "True Law of Population," he writes—" The great general law, then, which as it seems really regulates the increase or decrease, both of vegetable and animal life, is this—that whenever a species or genus is endangered, a corresponding effort is invariably made by nature for its preservation and continuance by an increase of fecundity or fertility, and that this especially takes place whenever such danger arises from a diminution of proper nourishment or food, so that consequently the state of depletion, or the deplethoric state, is favourable to fertility in the ratio of the intensity of each state, and this probably throughout nature universally, in the vegetable as well as the animal world; further, that as applied to mankind, this law produces the following consequences, and acts thus :—

"There is in all societies a constant increase going on amongst that portion of it which is the worst supplied with food, in short, amongst the poorest.

"Amongst those in a state of affluence and well supplied with food and luxuries, a constant decrease goes on. Amongst those that form the mean or medium between those two opposite states—that is to say, among those who are tolerably well supplied with good food, and not overworked nor yet idle— population is stationary. Hence it is upon the numerical proportion which these three states bear to each other in any society that increase or decrease upon the whole depends."

That is the complete statement which Mr. Doubleday collected statistics to prove, and very satisfactorily he proved it.

The most curious perversity of the human mind, is, however, instanced in Mr. J. S. Mill's "Political Economy," for in the note on page 197 of the sixth edition, he actually makes use of the peerage as affording evidence to contradict Mr. Doubleday, when, as the latter's readers will see, the peerage statistics are Mr. Doubleday's best proof; but Mr. Mill's remarks are only generalities concerning facts which generalities' statistics prove to be wrong.

Again, Mr. Mill refers with approval to Mr. Carey's remark that, if Doubleday's theory was correct, the increase of the population of the United States, apart from immigration, should be one of the slowest on record, showing therefore that he did not completely understand Mr. Doubleday; for Mr. Doubleday says particularly in the passage above quoted, not that diminution of sustenance is the only cause, but a chief one, and when, as in the case of America, hard work has produced the same depletive effect as lack of sustenance would do, and so a great increase of population, the increase merely proves Mr. Doubleday's theory true. The extra hard work entailed on man in such a case as America, causes a depletive effect which the capacity of the stomach cannot obviate by an equally rapid increase. The causes of the depletion may be many, and difficulty of getting food or hard work is one just as much as lack of food or sustenance. In all young colonies every one knows life is extremely hard, though equally also food is cheap and abundant.

Doubleday's views will be found fully developed by Herbert Spencer in his "Biology," sec. 343, &c., where the learned author explains the antagonism between development and genesis, or as we must put it, in Political Economy, between utility and reproduction. Darwin undoubtedly held the same views as Doubleday, but however fully confirmed, the idea would be ridiculed by some people.

The whole matter springs from the limit which has been placed upon all things; whether the limit is the limit of consumption or the limit of development, or anything else, the doctrine holds good, because of the limit.

Consumption is limited, but moves from the material towards the immaterial, therefore it stands to reason that the more consumption tends to become material, the less immaterial it is; but immateriality is the cause of reproductivity; consequently the more material, or the greater the utility of any object, the less is its effect in the reproduction of desire in others.

4. *Theory of the differentiation of consumption.*—We have so far traced, first, the cause of consumption, secondly, the cause of its increase, and now we come to the increase itself, and propose to show how, by the differentiation of the classes who consume into poor, middle, and rich, consumption is positively increased in volume, so that the total consumption of a community, among whom there is the greatest inequality of fortune, is greater than the total quantity consumed by those communities, whose individuals are upon a nearer equality in respect of wealth. And this is in effect to verify the statement so much laughed at by economists,

that the consumption of the rich is necessary to the labour of the poor, that because the rich consume more out of proportion to their diminished number, therefore their expenditure is more beneficial to the poorer classes than the expenditure of the poorer classes themselves.

Lawyers have accustomed the public to the words necessaries and superfluities in a practical manner; we do not mean to say that such terms were formerly unknown, but law has brought them within the range of practical economics, and considering consumption from this light, we may say that legal necessaries are the index of what we will call necessary consumption. The poorer classes, then, in any society, are limited to the consumption of necessaries, and the law limits the higher class, which comes under its domination, to the same class of consumption, and this may be taken as the middle or index of consumption; but, inasmuch as the consumption of the poorest of the poor never falls below this, whereas the consumption of the rich always rises above it, the consumption of the rich is greater in proportion than the consumption of the poor. We all of us know, that, given a certain station in life, a certain expenditure is necessary, and a higher income yields a disproportionate ability to consume: for instance, take an undergraduate at a university, given £200 a year, and he is in comfortable circumstances, add then but another £50, and the effect will be out of proportion to the increase; he will be in a position to spend upon superfluities more in proportion to the income; suppose that 10 per cent. of the former goes in superfluities, 15 per cent. of the latter will go. In the first case £20 will be spent, in the latter £37. 10s, instead of, as one would expect, £25. We all of us know and feel this to be so, yet few economists practically regard it.

But, again, suppose a Duke, with £365,000 a year, wants or takes a fancy to a fine pair of carriage horses, which are offered to him and bought for £1000, the Duke has here consumed as much as would pay, say 1000 labourers for a week at £1. Now can anyone suppose that 1000 men would devote a week's work simply that one of them, or one of them at a time, might enjoy the use of those horses? Such an idea seems ridiculous; consequently, if there was no Duke, there would not be the valuable horses, for there would be no one who could pay their price. This way of looking at the question is open to the objection, that the proportion between the number of Dukes and the number of labourers is in favour of the labourers; that is to say, that the extra number of labourers beyond the thousand would bring the consumption up to that of the highest classes. The better statement would be by taking the consumption of the richest and the poorest together, to see if it was greater than the

8 *

middle class. There is, however, no way of proving the matter by statistics in this manner, and the only way of proving it is by considering the proposition, that the further off the labour is, from us at the time of consumption, with the results of which we buy, the more readily do we part with the means of purchase, a fact so obvious as to need no comment. There are no persons so ready to spend as those who have never produced, but who have acquired their property by gift or devise, and it is this increasing readiness to spend which proves the differentiation and consequent increase of consumption.

There is, however, another matter to be considered, which calls for all an economist's care and attention. In young states, in progressive states, there exists this differentiation and consequent increase of consumption, but from a consideration of the true method of proving it to exist, namely, by taking the consumption of the highest and lowest together, and comparing it with the middle class consumption, an idea of importance is suggested, which is, that inasmuch as wealth, while differentiating the classes, has produced of its own accord by so doing an increasing middle class, and as this class tends ultimately to trench upon the other two, so wealth must ultimately get rid of the increase of consumption caused by its differentiation.

Now this is one of the most curious phenomena

of wealth, for it explains at once the cause of the decadence of wealth in a state. When the middle classes have, as we will suppose, made their consumption either to equal or surpass that of the lowest and highest put together, it stands to reason that there productivity of desire must cease to operate as powerfully as before, for the scope of its operation diminishes with the increasing uniformity of society.

The nearer approach we make to an equality in style of living and expenditure, the less effect that expenditure by one person must have on any other person, and as the reproductivity of desire dies out, so must wealth cease; for when we cease to desire we cease to labour or trouble ourselves to obtain, and with the increasing satisfaction increases the irksomeness of the labour.

The word division, as used by Adam Smith in relation to labour, is not nearly so expressive as differentiation, because it merely expresses the cause and not the effect, which is what it is desired to express. The object is not merely to divide society into three or more classes, but to note the effects of that division upon the consumption of the community. It is the smaller numbers of the upper classes that makes them richer, or perhaps we should say it is their riches that makes them smaller; but ultimately the poorer classes reap a benefit by their spending more and getting less in return than their poorer neighbours. By the differentiation of labour, the sum of the labour is reduced; by the differentiation of consumption, the sum of consumption is increased, and with it the labour and the classes who live thereby.

CHAPTER III.

SOME GENERAL REMARKS ON THE CONSUMPTION OF COMMODITIES.

1. *Of effective demand.*—It may perhaps seem at first sight absurd that we should devote a section merely to the discussion of what is or is not effective demand, but as a reader of the works of the objective economists, it seems to us that those writers have no clear idea of what is meant by these words, and the remarks we have made concerning Mill on excess of supply go to prove that Mill himself had but a very confused notion of what comes under the head of effective demand, for as we have shown, one of his most powerful arguments merely proves that there is ineffective demand, a fact of which everyone is certainly sufficiently aware.

This work on economy treats solely of effective demand, but because it does so it does not necessarily ignore the other sort of demand, but merely states that as regards this view of wealth we only argue upon the former.

The words effective demand import such a demand as is or has been satisfied. The fact of a man having bought a loaf of bread proves effective demand for a fixed quantity of bread, and therefore, until any given commodity is not only produced but has actually been bought or consumed, there is no such thing predicable as effective demand. Seeing, then, that effective demand relates solely to past facts, no supposition is permissible in an economical argument of what may or can be bought, so that such statements as the Free Trade party are wont to make on occasion, that if so and so can be produced cheaper, something else may be bought, are statements utterly irrelevant and outside the mark. They are statements with which this system of political economy has no possible concern; the question propounded by economy is not what may be, but simply what is and why it is, and from facts conclusions may be drawn.

Again, the ordinary works on economy will be found full of such statements as, that capital is the result of saving, and if we save we shall then be able to consume more, and our wealth will be increased; all such statements are similarly, however true they may be or be made to appear, utterly beyond the scope of this design.

Political Economy must proceed upon a fixed basis, and that fixed basis is the amount which either has been or is being consumed; with future consumption it cannot deal at all. It stands to reason, therefore, that effective demand is absolutely limited; that which is past cannot be altered.

2. *All effective is absolutely limited.*—This of course follows from what we have said above. If effective demand means that demand which is or has been satisfied, then it equally follows that that demand is limited.

It is a fact that between our getting up one morning and our getting up the following day, we have utilized or consumed a given number of articles or commodities, and although it may be true that my consumption on Tuesday is greater than that on Monday, yet inasmuch as regards one day the demand is fixed and limited, so as regards the two put together the demand is fixed and limited.

Now these remarks may seem both childish and absurd to many, too obvious to need comment, but, in the first place, it is from this absolute limit that the most important deductions may be drawn, and secondly, it will by many be hardly credited that Mill in his principles should regard these facts as not only untrue but almost unsupposable, for he writes at Book III, Chapter 14, sec. 3, "Thus in whatever manner the question (excess of supply) is looked at, though we go to the extreme verge of possibility to invent a supposition favourable to it, the theory of general overproduction implies an absurdity;" and what is this supposition which goes to the extreme verge of possibility? Further back in the same section he writes, "Assume the most favourable hypothesis for the purpose, that of a limited community, every member of which possesses as much of necessaries and of all known luxuries as he desires, and since it is not conceivable that persons whose wants were completely satisfied would labour and economize to obtain that which they did not desire: suppose a foreigner arrives, and produces an additional quantity of something of which there was already enough, here it will be said is over-production," &c., and then Mr. Mill goes on to say this is ill-assorted production, with which we have nothing to do just now. All we wish to call attention to is the curiosity of Mill's reasoning, when he talks about going to the verge of possibility.

The facts are just exactly what Mill supposes them hardly possible to be, namely, in a given time a limited community, with an absolutely limited demand, and so far from this being a favourable hypothesis, it is the only true and reasonable, that is capable of being reasoned upon, hypothesis, any other supposition being quite beside the question of economics. The fact is, that every community possesses as much of necessaries and of all known luxuries as it desires, that is, of course, effectively desires; it may desire more, but its desire for more is ineffective, and therefore is not desire so far as Political Economy is concerned.

3. *All our wants are satisfied.*—Here is another deduction so obvious as hardly to need comment,

and yet no proposition will be more strenuously denied by some. When we say all our wants are satisfied, we mean our effective demand. Effective demand means that demand which is or has been satisfied, therefore it stands to reason that our wants, so far as economy is concerned, are absolutely satisfied: it may seem absurd to say so, but it is none the less a fact.

It will then be seen from this, that the only question with which economy has to concern itself is the question how much is paid for the satisfaction, or, will the country benefit, supposing less is given to get that demand satisfied. *Prima facie* it stands to reason that the giving less to get our demand satisfied is no benefit, for if we get what we want, what matters it how much we pay for getting the commodity. If I want a carriage and pair, and get one, my paying less for it or more for it, so long as I get it, is of no great consequence to me; I have the carriage and that suffices.

But there is, however, another matter with which we have to deal, which seems quite unknown to the objective economist, namely, the question of saving for future consumption. Man is always looking forward to to-morrow. He is always trying to get for himself excess of supply, that is to say, doing so much to-day as will enable him to be idle to-morrow, or so much one year that the next year he may be able to enjoy life. Now this is the sort of excess of supply, or saving, which Mill's arguments do not seem to comprehend at all. If a man's effective demand to-day is x, and he produces $10x$, there is at once excess of supply, but, by the jumbling up of productive and reproductive consumption, Mill quite obliterates this; he supposes that what is not effectively demanded, for what we call productive consumption, to-day is consumed reproductively, and therefore no excess of supply is possible,—that if I want ten needles or pins, and twenty are produced, the extra ten will go to pay labour, whereas according to our view, even if they do go to pay labour, there is none the less excess of supply of commodities which are intended for productive consumption, which is the whole question. But this is rather travelling off the point.

The question of how much or how little we give to get our effective demand satisfied, depends entirely upon the question of effective demand for capital, and effective demand for capital depends upon what is really ineffective demand, that is, supposed demand. For instance, a certain set of men get together to construct a railway, and absorb capital in so doing now until the railway is actually finished and in use; or if it be a mine, the mine actually opened and the contents actually selling, there is no effective demand; the demand is merely supposed to exist, and the question whether or no the work will satisfy a want is one with which no known system of economy can deal. All it can deal with practically and usefully is the satisfactions when they have been proved to exist, by having been actually purchased and so rendered effective.

To most of our readers this will probably seem taking a very narrow and contracted view of the matter, and so it may possibly be; but it seems none the less the only view for which any sort of useful deductions can be got, besides which it separates or enables us more clearly to separate, and keep quite distinct, in our minds the difference between productive consumption—that is, that consumption which directly produces in man the sensation of satisfaction, and reproductive consumption, that consumption which may, but, so far as we know, does not, produce that sensation, save indirectly and through the medium of others.

4. *Effective demand constantly increasing.*—The facts alluded to above, that our effective demand is by its nature always limited and certain for any given time, does not, of course, militate against its perpetual increase any more than the fact that I eat a loaf of bread one morning prevents my eating more than that another morning; neither is it necessary for the supposition to suppose that population is limited, and can neither increase nor decrease. It may seem curious to say so, but as regards this argument, all increase takes place in what, for convenience sake,

we have called eternity: fix any limit of time, as that about which you are arguing, and it follows that any increase or decrease takes place afterwards, after time, the time you are speaking about. For instance, suppose we were to take the year 1880, then it is quite possible to state the exact number, neither more nor less by a fraction, of persons who lived during that period which we call 1880. We may do the same with 1881; but notwithstanding the positively fixed number of persons who lived during 1880, there has been an increase in the population; that increase, however, in respect of 1880 takes place in 1881, and yet as regards 1881, the population is equally fixed; so that if you took the two years together, you might say that there was no increase in population, any increase as regards that period being in 1882. The fact is, there is no increase whatever in time, and yet there is an increase, so that the only way out of the difficulty seems to be to use the word eternity as meaning that which is beyond time to express the idea.

Now the most favourite arguments in economy are those which deal with the increase of demand, because they go to show the supposed amelioration of man's condition by reducing the labour, and so enabling him to be more idle. The object of much thought is how to get the same result with less labour, the conclusion being that if we spend less labour in one way we shall get more things or commodities by utilizing this surplus labour, which, of course, is simply a *non sequitur;* for, as we have shown, our demand is absolutely fixed and positively satisfied, and, therefore, the saving of labour in one way does not prove its use in another.

By going back to what we said before concerning the increase in population, it is evident that, in order to truly state any proposition concerning the increase or decrease of anything, two factors must be considered. It is impossible to predicate of any given period, that there has been either an increase or a decrease in the population without the use of two factors.

When people say that there has been an increase in the population of any country in one year, their statement can only be possibly true upon the supposition that they meant there were more on the 31st of December than there were on the 1st of January of that year, that there is an excess by comparing two periods together. The expression that the increase is in any given year is elliptical, and what is intended is, that as regards the preceding year, the population of the one in question shows an increase. This, then, although not perhaps so clear as we should like to have made it, shows that in any question concerning increase of wealth there are two factors to consider, and that, assuming our supposition true, that wealth is commodities consumed, therefore it is not merely necessary to prove greater ease of production, but also a positively greater consumption in proportion to prove increase of wealth, a thing which most writers fail to prove.

Now, it is generally conceded that money is the measure of wealth, and that, as Professor Fawcett says, when a man is said to be worth £100,000, you are merely stating the quantity of goods, wares, and merchandize he possesses. For the sake, then, of explaining the laws of increase, as we shall call them for convenience sake, we take this for granted as being true of money.

Now, it is usually the case that a measure operates directly, and that when you say, for instance, a piece of cloth has more yards in it than another piece of cloth, you mean that there is more cloth actually. It may, however, be possible that money, unlike all other measures, operates inversely, and that the more valuable or the higher the price, the smaller is the quantity of wealth contained in, or represented by, the article whose wealth you are measuring. It is, of course, possible to conceive that if a gold watch could be bought for 6*d*, there would be more wealth as measured by money than if the same watch had cost us £60. Now, the great difficulty about the matter is to know what money measures; what is it in the watch which we, according to the objective economists, measure by money? The watch does not get smaller, or lighter, or narrower, or a different colour, because it is shown by the measure to be either less or more wealth. Wealth, they say, is a quality in the watch; why, then, we ask, does the measure show a variation in the watch, and yet the watch does not show it? The only conclusion we can draw from this argument seems to be that money is not a measure; but Mr. J. S. Mill says it is—see "Political Economy," vol. ii., page 3, *et seq.* So that we are put in a great dilemma.

If, then, to suit the objective economists, money is a measure which operates inversely, and the greater the price the less is the wealth, of course it follows that a dust heap is more wealth than the same-sized heap of diamonds. which is a conclusion too absurd to contemplate or discuss.

Money, then, is a measure which acts like all other measures directly, therefore it follows that the less price we pay for an article the less is the wealth contained in, or represented by, the article.

Let us, then, apply this to the increasing consumption of commodities. If the price of a commodity is lowered, say 20 per cent., then the commodity is shown to contain less wealth, just in the same way as by cutting off 20 yards from 100 yards of cloth, the cloth which remains is less by 20 yards.

But now, supposing, in the case of the cloth, we knew that every time we cut a bit off the cloth the cloth would grow again, should we then be justified in saying the more we cut off the more cloth we must get, because it grows? Certainly not; the idea would at once occur to us that unless what grew was more in proportion to the quantity we cut off, we should soon exhaust our cloth.

Similarly with regard to our wealth. We know perfectly well that every reduction of price causes an increasing demand, but what we do not know is how much increased demand will arise upon every diminution of price; and, therefore, just as in cutting off our cloth we should soon exhaust our stock did not the cloth grow at least in proportion to what we cut off, so it is no use to suppose that a mere cutting off of price will increase the wealth of the country.

If 1000 yards of cotton sheeting, which, say, originally cost 6d a yard or £25, are, by the introduction of Free Trade, reduced in price to 4d a yard, then it follows, if money be a measure, that there is less wealth in the 1000 yards by $33\frac{1}{3}$ per cent., but more than 1000 yards will now be consumed; the question arises how much, and it is answered by the statement that there must be at least £25 worth of cotton sheeting, or $333\frac{1}{3}$ yards more consumed, in order that there may be as much wealth as before, *ergo*, the Free Trade theory is a *non sequitur*, provided that money be admitted to be a measure.

5. *The fact that we do not consume proves that we do not want.*—This is almost a re-statement of the preceding one, that our wants are all satisfied; but we are compelled to discuss the matter to some extent

again in consequence of what we have said concerning the constant increase of effective demand, for it is not exactly our business to consider the question of increasing demand. So far as economy is concerned, the fact that we do not obtain shows that we do not want; no doubt it seems hard to say so, but it is the only firm ground upon which any scientific truths may be constructed.

The question of whether a country will benefit by getting its wants satisfied with greater ease is one of great difficulty, and depends entirely upon the condition of progress which the society has made in civilization. In a case of progressive civilization, when we know as a fact what Locke has told us, that the greater good will not move the will (that is, economically, will not cause greater effective demand), it stands to reason that greater difficulty of obtaining satisfaction is the only means of promoting wealth, that is, of causing effective demand. Man must be made uneasy in order to convince him that the handsome conveniences of life are better than nasty penury.

Objective economists always beg the question (which really is, do we effectively demand, or in the case of increase, how may we be made to effectively demand?) by supposing that the every production proves an effective demand when we have good reason to know it proves nothing of the sort; and in order to avoid this obvious *petitio principii*, it is necessary to state positively that consumption alone proves effective demand—that is, effective demand for productive consumption; that is that consumption which provides for the consumer satisfaction. As, therefore, consumption is the only proof of fact which we can avail ourselves of, we are compelled to say, though it may seem very harsh, that the fact that we do not consume is a proof that we do not want or effectively demand.

6. *Of the proof of effective demand.*—That which anyone gives for a thing is proof of his effectively demanding that thing; for instance, if we buy a loaf of bread, that is proof positive of our wanting the loaf, and not only is this the case, but the argument must be also regarded as quantitively true—that is to say, that the quantity I pay is the proof of the amount of my demand, and not merely of the demand.

This is a most important fact to be understood, for it proves at once that all exchange involves excess of supply, and also that the smaller the quantity which is offered in exchange, the greater is the excess of supply.

Not only, then, is our having bought a loaf of bread proof of our effective demand for bread, but if we have given $4d$ for the loaf, that $4d$ measures our effective demand for the loaf.

Carrying this principle into that of exchange, we see at once that, whereas in the case of consumers the supply and demand are always equal, in the case of producers they never are equal, for supply is always in excess, and by quoting the axiom of Euclid, that if unequals be added to equals the sum is unequal, we show at once that there is always excess of supply.

The producers and consumers we will suppose exchange pins for needles; if, then, the consumer gives ten needles and get ten pins in exchange, no one can say that he has either gained or lost, for it must be supposed that what he gave was the exact measure of his demand, and therefore in his view he must have got at least as much as he gave; probably he thinks he got more, but for the sake of argument we will suppose that the supply and demand are here equal. But the producer could not continue to produce and exchange unless what he got was more than what he gave,—surely this will be admitted,—and inasmuch as what he got, ten needles, are by *others* valued at more than what he gave, ten pins, and as what he gave is evidence of his effective demand, so he must have got an excess of supply. Therefore all exchange involves excess of supply beyond effective demand.

Now there is no way so obvious in order to produce and increase excess of supply as to limit it (the supply); such is the paradoxicality of economics. For if a consumer endeavours to obtain an article, the greater the difficulty of getting it the greater must be the effort, or the result of it, which is necessary to induce the producer to part with it, and were it not for competition, producers would always be, as it were, hanging fire with their productions in order to stimulate the struggles of consumers to obtain, for the result of such struggling when turned into commodities goes ultimately into the producer's pocket.

Now to many readers it will seem as if in the above arguments both parties were equally producers and consumers, and that Mr. Mill's dictum, that all consumers are *ex vi termini* producers, was true; but inasmuch as exchange involves excess of supply, and as that excess is available for purchase, all consumers are not fairly said to be *ex vi termini* producers, for the consumer *may have been* a producer, he need not necessarily *be* one at the time of exchange, and unless he is, it is not fair to say all consumers are *ex vi termini* producers, for such a statement disregards time, and is one of what we call the eternity statements objective economists are so fond of.

It is by means of this proved excess of supply that the theory of this differentiation and consequent increase of effective demand is proved to exist, for this excess of supply is just what the man who has so obtained his means of purchase is so ready to part with, and which consequently is used to increase his effective demand.

All these questions about effective demand and its measurement, are root questions which objectionists slur over, but if they are, as it seems to us, they must be admitted to be true; then objective economy fails completely in its arguments. If money is the measure of effective demand and of wealth, then it stands to reason money proves conclusively inequality in exchange. If, however, it does not do so, then we should be very glad to know what it does, for it becomes useless as a medium of exchange, unless it measures the quality of the things exchanged.

7. *The demand of the poor will not employ them.*— This is one of the most difficult points in economics, for it is the root question proposed by Mr. George in his " Progress and Poverty." It is a fact well known as to need no comment, that people will not exchange unless advantage prompts them, and it requires no very astute mind to perceive that in the case of the poor of any country, the advantage is so small, we might almost say so non-existent, as to prevent exchange. If A can get nothing by making chairs for B, A will not do it, and the only way to enable him to get anything in the way of profit is for his effective demand to be smaller than that of B; but the poor are so poor that the effective demand being limited to the very smallest quantity which will support life, it becomes absolutely and

physically impossible to make any difference, and so any profit by exchange.

If the system of the objective economists were true, it would of course follow that poverty could not exist for the reverse of the reason given above; that is to say, no excess of supply being possible, and no profit being therefore got from exchange, exchange becomes a mere philanthropic proceeding for providing Jacques and Jean with a greater number of commodities; but unfortunately filthy lucre prompts exchange just as it prompts labour, and no exchange can possibly take place without it. Therefore, where the effective demand of all classes is equal, no profit is possible and no exchange either.

It seems to follow that the only way out of the difficulty lies in communism, which however is simply going out of the frying pan into the fire, for under communism the only result would be man's struggles to produce inequality by idleness, which would be fatal to any progress.

The great object of the State should be to endeavour to produce inequality among those poor people somehow, and the moment that was done the wheels of society would begin to go round.

Compulsory labour and payment by the State is only a method of increasing poverty, for it enables those to live who would otherwise be got rid of by the survival of the fittest.

The want of progress inherent in the lower orders of society is a most perplexing problem, and while utterly disagreeing with those who, like Mr. George, suppose robbery of the rich will ameliorate the condition of the poor, we confess we are unable to solve the problem.

Probably no one has done more to injure Ireland than Mr. Gladstone, though of course he is about the last person who would either desire it or admit it. For from the reasons given above, it will be seen that taking away from the rich is just the very thing of all others to injure the poor, for the expenditure of the rich is the employment of the poor, and however much we may desire to benefit the poor, yet the desire which all men have to get a profit is quite sufficient of itself to prevent any scheme from succeeding which relies for its efficacy upon robbing Peter to pay Paul. If differentiation or inequality is the cause of progress, then the greater the inequalities of fortune, the greater will be the progress, and the only method of enriching Ireland is to introduce inequality, by getting rid of small holdings and the grovelling of equality. What is wanted is a differentiation of classes into the day labourer, the farmer, the operative, the merchant and manufacturer, and the landlord, instead of a State where all strive to rule and none obey.

8. *Of the inverse ratio of supply and demand.—*

Speaking generally we may say that the greater the supply of any article, the less we want it, and the less we are therefore disposed to give for it. From the producer's point of view this is a most important matter, for it follows from this that every restriction of production is an increase of profit, more commodities must be given to pay for a less amount of commodities, and so the fact that producers go on producing is not proof, as Mill supposes, of a growing, but of a decreasing demand, that is to say, less is being given and more is being got, and if less is being given there is less demand.

While we are on this question we have a word to say about supply and demand generally. If Mr. Mill had grasped his opponent's view fully, he would have seen that when he was arguing against what they call excess of supply, he ought to have laid himself out to prove that excess of demand was an irrational and absurd doctrine, for that which a subjective economist calls excess of supply is objectively excess of demand, and not supply. Commodities pay for commodities, but the commodities which buy, that is the demand commodity, is always in excess in any exchange, of the supply commodity, but, inasmuch as people talk subjectively, and as a commodity is a commodity in respect of man, it follows that this excess of demand is really an excess of supply. Objectively there is an excess of demand, but subjectively it is called excess of supply. Supposing two men to require the one a pound of beef for a day's consumption, and the other a pound of bread for a similar period, then if the one gave one and a half pounds of bread, and got one pound of beef in exchange, there would be an excess of supply of bread, half a pound more bread than was necessary, but this excess of supply arises in the exchange, because the man is demanding beef more imperatively than the other man is demanding bread, his demand is in excess, so that here there is an excess of demand of bread, but subjectively and altruistically we call it an excess of supply.

Seeing then that both the supply and demand of any commodity is always limited, and also that the supply is always equal to the demand and generally greater than it, it follows that if you take away one, the other is greater in proportion.

If the demand for nails in a week is ten thousand, and in that time twelve thousand are produced, the producers, in struggling to get rid of that extra two thousand, will lower the demand in proportion to the increase in the supply, and although more being produced does actually limit the consumption, yet it does so potentially, for the amount paid in goods for what is consumed is lessened, and thereby at the same time is the producer's power of consumption reduced.

Although, however, this is generally the case, it is not so entirely true as may at first sight be supposed.

It is sometimes the case, for instance, that a reduction in the price of a two-penny paper, from two-pence to a penny, will more than double the circulation of it, and when it does so the demand increases with the supply; but this is really a very exceptional case, and could we half the price of everything to-morrow, it is plain we should not by doing so double the consumption.

We cannot but admit but this is a most puzzling question in economics, and one which practice is able to solve far better and easier than theory, for in any question of theory where exchange is involved, it becomes difficult to see that what is called excess of supply, is objectively, that is, from the point of view of exchange, excess of demand, or perhaps we should not say that it is so difficult to see, as so difficult to follow out argumentatively.

It follows, then, that a restricted production is beneficial to producers, and were it not for competition, they would make consumers to suffer from their greediness, but competition altruism steps in and produces just the very opposite effect which was anticipated; in the struggle to get a living from production, production always tends to excess, and a consequent reduction of profit all round. Consumers by hanging fire, or repressing their desires, are enabled to buy cheap, and so to reduce the excessive profits which producers might obtain by a combination to restrict the output.

*See Errata on back page

CHAPTER IV.

OF THE MEANS BY WHICH WE ARE ENABLED TO CAUSE A CONSTANTLY INCREASING EFFECTIVE DEMAND.

1. *Man's wants are never satisfied.*—This heading of a fresh chapter seems like a direct contradiction of section 1 of the last chapter, and so it undoubtedly is. Man is but a mass of contradictions, and he who sits down to write about man had almost best set out his propositions and their proofs, merely that he may be able to knock them down again with fresh arguments, drawn from the reverse view of his original propositions.

Our first proposition, that all our wants were satisfied, will receive as much of opposition as this will receive of assent, and so ready will the assent be to this, that to argue in support of it seems both superfluous and unnecessary. Yet it is necessary to explain and enforce this as much as the other view of the matter, because it is this which stirs us up to fresh and renewed exertions in pursuit of wealth.

It is a current saying that the more we have the more we want, and as a current saying it carries conviction, for no sayings which become and remain current contain untruth, and this great truth is recognized in the saying *Vox populi vox Dei.* The public as a public are always right, and he who appeals to them, and succeeds in his appeal without creating a bias, is the wisest of men. It is of course the case that there are both paradoxists and followers, and believers in paradoxes, but in the long run they only render themselves subjects for the shafts of ridicule and butts for the majority to aim their wit at. And the persecutions of those who have been esteemed wise beyond their generation may be regarded as the outcome of a feeling, that those wise men were really leading the people along a path of error, the outcome of an instinctive feeling that such knowledge was attended with no good result *at the time.*

Regard the matter how we will, no one save perchance a few philosophers are ever satisfied, and even with the philosophical it is merely a transfer of uneasiness from the material to the immaterial, from the bodily uneasiness to the uneasiness of the mind or soul. Turn where we may " man never is but always to be blest," and it is this feeling that, regarding from a bodily or material point of view, is that which is perpetually urging man to increase his wealth or material satisfactions.

It may not seem out of place, then, if we set down a few of the means which man possesses of causing this uneasiness, for some means he undoubtedly possesses which conduce to that object, and within limits those means may be utilized, we say within limits, for the fact that wealth has a limit is just as true as that man has a limited effective demand, in fact the two ideas are synonymous. If we have no effective demand, then we cannot have any wealth.

When we say man has a means of causing uneasiness, and so producing the struggles necessary to produce wealth, we think that this will be found to be one of the great points of difference between man and animals; no animals ever struggle to progress, they lack the perception of the immaterial, which causes progress in knowledge or wealth or anything else. Man knows that obstacles are essential to progress, and he alone puts obstacles in his own path, that by the overcoming of them he may increase his knowledge or his wealth, or his ability to obtain his desires. It seems to us that this is the interpretation to put upon the account in Scripture of the tree of the knowledge of good and evil; that account is sufficient to give the clue to progress; as long as we are without the knowledge of evil, good, that is the greater good, moves not the will.

2. *Of the increase and change of desire.*—In the preceding part of this treatise we said that man's wants were not only always satisfied, that is from the point of view of Political Economy, but that they were always more than satisfied, that there is inherent in every mercantile exchange, or in the majority of

exchanges on the market, a profit, and that that profit was really nothing more than excess of supply of means of satisfying those wants which are satisfied in any given period.

Now it is of course clear, that, if there were no means whatever of utilizing this excess of supply, the markets would be in a perpetual state of glut, and men would cease work till the excess of supply had been productively consumed.

Providence, however, has, as it were, forestalled the idleness which would result by such over-production, and has, by constantly causing an increase of desire, or in many cases a change of desire, enabled man to utilize this surplus.

The fact that more corn is produced in any one year than is consumed, or, as we might put it, the price having compelled a surplus to revert to the producers, has, by so doing, enabled the producers to consider the question of the supply of some other of man's wants, and the fact of his increasing ability to do this is apt to cause an increase in the desire of the consumer; not only an increase, however, commonly results, but a mere change in the form of desire, and this change is called fashion, which may be defined as the pursuit of the immaterial in *another* material form.

This constant increase and change of desire is very apt to give rise in the ideas of an objective economist to the supposition that supply and demand are equalized, but the producer having originally got a surplus is not so foolish as to give that surplus up for nothing, and gets in the result a fresh excess of supply.

Desire, however, and in consequence, always reaches saturation point, that is the time when we really cease to effectively demand, sooner than the producers cease to produce, and this for the obvious reason of profit, and the necessary consequence follows that producers have remaining on their hands a surplus, which they are unable for a time to utilize. They become like the schoolboy, home for the Christmas holidays, gorged with an excess which they find it extremely hard to digest and reproductively employ; their own desire for profit is the ultimate cause of the stagnation.

It is a fact, too, often forgotten by economists, that man's effective desires are absolutely limited just as the capacity of his stomach, and that no amount of arguing will urge him to procure things for which he does not really care. That consequently there is, notwithstanding Mill's assertion to the contrary, an absolute limit on the quantity of capital which can be reproductively employed in any given time and in every known community; that to say with Mill that capital is capable of giving unlimited employment to industry is simply untrue. Man's wants are limited though increasing, and the capital employed in producing satisfactions is consequently limited though increasing.

3. *Protection considered subjectively both egoistically and altruistically.*—We need hardly at this distance through the book remind the reader that the system here explained is founded upon the consideration of mind and matter, and that being so, it is essential to an understanding of the reason why, of any question to seek for it in mind as well as in matter, and that if a good reason can be got from mind, the argument from matter may be disregarded.

Mr. John Stuart Mill, the greatest exponent of objective economy, says, in his essay on "The Definition and method of Political Economy," that to treat of mind and matter is both incongruous and absurd, and we may infer from this that his arguments will be such as to endeavour to beg the question of mind, for his subject deals with both, as his essay admits: we mention this that the reader may more clearly understand why the following arguments are used in regard to protection. They are arguments which, by taking a slight survey of mind, prove conclusively what is the use of protection from a mental point of view, and because it is the case in economy that a given form of mind causes a given form of matter, no material arguments are available to upset the reasons here given. But it is a fact that the material arguments have in a great measure shown conclusively that protection is a good.

The mental argument necessary to prove the truth of a protectionist policy, is simply that given by John Locke, and quoted above, namely, that good, the greater good, moves not the will but uneasiness.

It is absolutely essential to the existence of wealth that a given form of mind should be produced, it is necessary that we should not only desire, but desire effectively; men sitting in a chair and wishing for a share of the 3 per cents. will not, however hard we may wish, produce the means of obtaining a portion of those coveted securities.

Locke, then, has told us what is obvious to most of us, that the greater good will not make us wish to obtain it, and if the greater good will not make us wish to obtain it, how can it be expected that the production of yards of cotton shirting will make us wish to obtain them. If what philosophers call somewhat vaguely, it must be admitted, the greater good, is not sufficient, is it to be supposed that reels of cotton will do it? We hardly think so. Again, not only is it necessary to move the will, it is necessary also in respect of Political Economy to move it to such an extent as to make us use force or strive to obtain the thing. Is it, then, to be supposed that the sight of a bale of cotton is sufficient to produce this further effect on our minds?

But there is a third limitation in the matter; not only has the bale of cotton got to move our will, not only must it move it so far as to cause us to exert ourselves, but it has also got to force us to find some mode of satisfying some one else's desires; surely one would think this last limitation would suffice to prevent our will from making any move in the matter at all, and that it has a great effect in limiting our desires is obvious to the most superficial student of economy.

This will, to any careful reader, seem a good deal for an exponent of economy to beg. Take a poor man in the street with very limited means; he sees a rich man driving by in his carriage, and thinks he should like to be in the rich man's shoes. Now regard all the steps that are taken in this case, and you will see that Free Traders beg a good deal of the question.

First, the man has to be convinced that a carriage is a good thing; this he possibly may not be.

Second, he has, after being so convinced, to make up his mind that the struggles he will have to make to get a carriage will not cost him so much as to more than compensate for the pleasure of the possession of a carriage, which he probably will not be; and,

Third, he must find some means of pleasing or providing satisfaction for some one else, or he cannot get the carriage—which he very likely will not be able to do.

And all these points Mr. J. S. Mill, following Adam Smith, begged in order to prove the folly of his ancestors in founding the mercantile system.

Protection here steps in and says, that as the good in the shape of the carriage has not moved this person's will, we must set to work to move it, and the means we will use will be those of rendering the person uneasy for want of the carriage.

Now many will think a concrete or individual case would here be in point, but it is impossible for us to put one, as protection always acts through the other person or altruistically; and in the case given above it would act by depriving the owner of the carriage of the carriage in effect, though, of course, not in substance, it would render it more difficult for the owner of the carriage to get it, that so the individual who was supposed to want one would be able to find a way of getting a carriage, namely, by assisting the supposed owner of the carriage to get one.

It is in consequence of our having to regard matters from the point of view of exchange, or altruistically, that renders any explanation so apparently complicated and incomprehensible. The object at which Protection aims is to benefit one man at the expense of another, as it were, and at the same time it denies the injury to the other. In the first place, it renders the obtaining of commodities by the rich more difficult, while at the same time it provides the poor with a means of assisting the rich to obtain; so that it actually benefits the poor, but it does not really injure the rich, for it enables him or, rather does not prevent him, from obtaining, and by increasing the difficulty raises his intelligence at the same time that it causes him to benefit the poor. This, we admit, is a complicated and perhaps to many incomprehensible statement, but because difficult to understand and hard to explain, it is not therefore untrue. Given the end, which we contend is the object of wealth, then both rich and poor benefit. Assuming that wealth has no object, then the poor benefit more than the rich are injured, and this because of the theory of the differentiation of consumption, for the increasing ability of the rich to obtain is sufficient to obviate to a great extent the injury done, or on this view supposed to be done, to them, though of course by regarding the end there is no injury at all. Inasmuch, then, as by disregarding the end we are still enabled to see that the poor are benefitted more than the rich are injured, so we see that even from the lowest view protection obtains the greater good for the greater number.

4. *Protection from the view of exchange or objectively considered.*—In young and progressive States the

effective demand is very small as everybody knows, and also the means of satisfying it are generally abundant, a fact noted by Mr. Carey in his supposed refutation of Doubleday.

In cases of this kind it follows that the desire for exchange of commodities is very small. What use can any consumer, whose wants are few and easily satisfied, find from exchange, when the means of personally satisfying his wants is ready to hand, and when he sees that the person with whom he is to exchange, who we call the producer, is sure to get a profit from that exchange? If I can get what I want without some one else, why should I be so philanthropic as to benefit that some one else instead of myself?

As society advances, however, we find our ability to procure our own satisfaction falls off, and we have to rely upon some one else to provide what we are then unable to get, or which the other person can procure more easily than ourselves.

In proportion, however, as society remains in the condition first alluded to, progress is rendered slow and difficult, for there is but small profit or surplus obtainable to devote to reproductive employment or the increase and satisfaction of new forms of desire. If we refuse to benefit others we ultimately fail in getting any benefit ourselves, and life seems to consist of a struggle between the endeavour to benefit ourselves without benefitting others, and the endeavour to benefit others without injury to self.

In consequence then, of the predominant egoism of uncivilized man, progress becomes impossible, and therefore protection has been introduced for the purpose of subjectively and objectively repressing it. It prevents uniformity in production, that is in the production of our satisfactions, by means of compulsory multiformity of production of the objects which give us those satisfactions. It says in effect it is not good to be alone. By protecting one set of goods, it compels more of another sort to be given in exchange to buy them; by restricting the production of one, it increases the production of the other, and by so doing enlarges the scope for, and the means of reproductive employment. It increases the amount of objective consumption, that is what is given in exchange, while it stimulates by a profit the desire for objective production.

A concrete explanation, however, is simpler. Suppose laws were to be introduced into this country to-morrow, to protect corn or agriculture, what would happen? The price of bread would rise, and what does that mean economically?—simply that more cotton goods from Manchester must be produced to buy it with. Would the country starve because bread was dearer? by no means. The fact that bread is dearer simply increases the amount of the disposable capital of the country, and that extra capital would be employed in procuring cheaper supplies of bread and in buying more of other things. To suppose that dearer bread would not create an outcry would be absurd, but it would very soon be allayed, because there would be increased means of buying it at the same time. By asserting equality in exchange, the most important question in economy is begged, the question of reproductive employment of the capital. It becomes necessary to invent a new meaning to the word save in order to make up for the discrepancy between facts and theory, and to assume an equally effective demand from all persons, and then to propound the startling paradox that half the world is voluntarily injuring itself for the benefit of the other half.

If the agriculture of this country was just sufficiently protected to keep it going at a profit, the profit would be spent in many ways just like any other profit would be spent, and the manufacturers must benefit. The destruction of the agricultural interests of this country by Cobden, although benefitting his friends for a time, will ultimately, by driving away their customers, injure them. If agriculture is injured to suit the whims of manufacturers, manufacturers must suffer from loss of customers to buy their goods, or, which is the same, from the customers having lost the means of purchase. But objectivists tell us that producers do not want customers, that a demand for commodities is not a demand for labour, or, which is the same, that we are always trying to get things we don't want, so we must be content simply to state our objective views from inequality of exchange.

5. *Of the middle man.*—Bearing in mind what we have said previously concerning excess of supply, and the fact that contracted production increases it, and considering that the competition of individuals is perpetually tending to increase production, it will of course follow that this excess of supply is always decreasing, for competition overcomes the prudential restraint of a monopoly.

It will, then, be not out of place if we call attention to the means which the evolution of society takes to obviate this evil result, and it will perhaps surprise our readers when we say that the excess is kept up by means of middle men, by greater rapidity of transmutation of goods consequent upon the interposition of more dealers or agents between the producers and the consumers, causing thereby greater rapidity of consumption.

It is, in fact, a means of operating in a different manner for a similar result as is obtained by protection. It increases the excess of supply, and so increases the objective reproduction or the productive employment of capital.

The producer having got by exchange an excess of supply, endeavours as soon as possible to get rid of that excess by a second exchange, in order to obtain capital in the form necessary for producing some fresh commodity. In early stages of society where communication is difficult, it is in consequence correspondingly easy to get rid of this excess, for the difficulty of communication renders it difficult for any middle man to form a just notion of the wants of the society in which he trades, and he consequently is more ready to take the excess from the producer's hands.

But as communication by degrees renders the perception of the amount of excess stronger in the mercantile community, it causes a greater fall in value, and a consequent increasing reduction of the excess, for value is the measure of excess. People, therefore, become less and less ready to buy the excess, both in consequence of its more clear perception and its greater tendency to decrease, by which means producers find it increasingly hard to part with the excess.

This consequently causes a third class of men to spring up, namely, the middle men, who take this excess from producers and hold it back, as it were, from consumers, so as in effect to increase the consumption by increasing the market over which it is spread.

The middle man is, as it were, a dealer in time, for he takes what producers cannot sell to-day in order that he may sell it to consumers to-morrow.

A word of caution to critics and readers is here perhaps necessary and beneficial, because it explains the difference between subjective and objective economy. Wealth does not depend upon quantity of objects as many suppose, but quantity of subjects, not on the number of things we have, but on the quantity of our effective desire for those things. Consequently, although in old time the excess of supply is smaller in quantity of objects, or in the number, say of pins and needles exchanged, yet in respect 1 of the greater desire and 2 of the greater ignorance of excess, the excess of old time is greater than the excess of modern days. If money price and value are the measures of wealth, then the excess of former times is greater than the excess at present; but if money price and value are either not measures or are measures by inverse ratio, then we give up all argument concerning economy. The reader then must not suppose that, because there is now a greater excess of objects than used to be, therefore we are merely denying facts when we state the excess of supply to be smaller. The very fact of there being a greater excess of objects is proof positive almost of a smaller excess of commodities.

This spreading of consumption is another cause of its increase, because it enables us to hold it, the thing produced, in suspense, and all commodities held in suspense are increased power of purchase. The fact of the middle man holding the goods enables him to spend. But it will be answered the consumption is simply transferred from the ultimate consumer; not so, however, for the middle man is spending to-day what the ultimate consumer would not spend till to-morrow.

The middle man compresses the eternity of consumption, or the future consumption, into the time, that is, the present moment, and so increases it, he forestalls but does not take away the ultimate consumer's power of consuming.

The consuming public, or, we should say, the public in respect of their consuming capacity, always and naturally object to the middle man; but there is no doubt he does a great service economically,—that is, one might say, as respects the producers, he enables them to produce continuously, which competition would tend to render intermittent, and by making it continuous he benefits the poorer classes who live by their labour. At the same time also he enlarges the public consumption, for it is a thing well known by the mercantile community that people who have goods, either actually or potentially, have in reality a greater power of purchase than those goods represents—they are in effect able to get credit by means of them for more than their actual value, and that sometimes as much as twice their value is put into their owners, or, we should say, mortgagee's hands, to be employed as he sees fit.

*See Errata on back page

BOOK III.

The Objective View of Wealth—Production.

CHAPTER I.

OF THE REQUISITES IN THE PRODUCTION OF COMMODITIES.

1. *Explanatory.*—The word wealth has been explained fully previously, so that any further explanation would seem unnecessary, but in consequence of the method of division here adopted, we have been obliged to so far misuse the word as to talk of objective wealth. Speaking correctly wealth is not an objective word at all, but a subjective one; in consequence, however, of the subjective altruistic method of looking at it, which is consequent upon wealth viewed from the light of exchange, it has almost become and is usually regarded both by the public who think a little and the writers on

Economy as an objective word. So strongly has this view dominated all thought, that we have been obliged, in deference to others in some measure, to pervert the meaning of the word.

It is a most curious thing in thought that in many cases, as Tennyson has remarked, second thoughts are not the best, and no word in the language has suffered so much from second thoughts as the word wealth. Ask a person who knows nothing whatever about economy, and you will see his first impulse in answering is to make the word a subjective one; give him time to think twice and he will then tell you in effect that it is an objective word.

But enough has been said concerning words.

The reader will have seen that in treating of subjective wealth, the object to keep steadily in view is the increase of consumption. The consumption of commodities is one of the greatest benefits to the human race, as a civilizer and a means of progress; and the true economist should therefore take it as his duty to strive by all means in his power to increase it. Consumption has its objects, and the object being good and not evil, its increase must be desired.

Now, however, in treating of objective wealth, or of commodities themselves, our ideas and views must of course be to some extent reversed, for though this latter view depends upon the former, and is subject to it, yet it becomes almost impossible to view production in any other light than its increase, so that we must treat the matter from the current view of economy, namely, with the object of the production of the greatest possible quantity of things to be consumed, and of the means by which, such as machinery and the division of labour, more commodities may be procured for consumption.

Inasmuch as the object of all economy, as it is somewhat falsely called, is consumption, the greater the number of things produced, the greater become the possibilities of consumption, and therefore our object in treating the matter objectively, is (pardon the tautology) objects.

It must however be borne in mind, that the greater number of commodities produced, does not prove the greater desire to consume; that, because production, always and perpetually, by means of exchange, outruns our effective demand, therefore, the blind-eyed increase of production is no necessary increase of wealth, in fact it amounts, as is shown by price, to a positive decrease. It decreases the quantity of capital which is being produced, it causes idleness amongst the very classes to whom labour is essential to existence, and in fact it is productive of innumerable evils, too far spreading to be entirely enumerated, or to be mentioned here otherwise than generally.

This system is constructed on the plan of making

price the measure of wealth directly, and therefore it shows that a falling market is a sure sign of overproduction in either one of two ways, either overproduction, more clearly perceived beyond productive consumption, or effective demand, or secondly an overproduction, not merely beyond productive consumption, but beyond reproductive consumption also.

It may perhaps not be out of place if we make here a few remarks upon the division of this treatise. It will surprise many, no doubt, that the section so fully developed by Messrs. Mill and Fawcett, headed distribution, is entirely absent. It seems to us that this division is both unnecessary and erroneous, for what do you understand by distribution but property?

Regarding wealth in the light of objective economy, no other meaning seems to be intended, and looking to the table of contents of their books, no other meaning seems to be attached by the writers to the word save, possibly, in the case of wages. Looking at the matter in the light of subjective economy, the idea conveyed by distribution means nothing if not property, for how can one treat of the galvanic distribution of satisfactions save under the idea of property in the commodity. The important question of the wages of labour, as it should be discussed under distribution, is, it seems to us, but a view of property in the results of labour, a subject treated to a small extent, in legal books, under the head of liens, or the right of individual to retain the thing which embodies the results of his labour until he receives his reward, payment or wages. It is perfectly true that in things treated of under the law of lieu, the matter in which the labour is embodied, is generally a valuable piece of property which has been given to the labourer, or entrusted to his care, for its safe keeping, but the fact, that the law of liens is not carried into every form of labour, seems to arise either from the fact that the division of labour has reduced every individual work to a minimum of utility, consequently reducing the value of a lien, or to the far greater injury which would result to trade and traders, from the ability of the workman to withhold, than the benefit which would result to the workman by a lien, if he had one. This being the view we take of the matter, the discussion of distribution comes in incidentally to every other discussion, so that no separate treatment seems at all necessary or essential; in fact, as the reader will see, we have classed it as one of the causes of the increase of production.

Wages merely mean satisfactions which have been expressed in money or objectively satisfactory objects given in exchange for labour, so that wages may safely be treated of under the heads of either property, labour, or exchange, and as regards their rise and fall should come under the latter, for the

11*

*See Errata on back page

rise and fall depends for its effect upon exchange, for it is conceivable that a man, who gets a penny a day, might be better off really than one who gets a pound in the same time.

Moreover, it would be taking a very narrow view of exchange, to say that it only means exchange of objects, and that a labourer* does perform an exchange when he gives his labour for wages.

2. *Of the requisites for the production of commodities.*—Upon what are and what are not the requisites for the production of commodities, most writers, thinkers and speakers will probably disagree. There is, in the whole range of Political Economy, no point or question which is not controverted both scientifically and polemically, and this particular question is no exception to the general rule. For the purpose of more fully settling the matter, we have divided the question into two, in the hope that such division will enable the reader to render a more ready assent to our view of the matter.

Of the requisites for the production of commodities, in the lowest and broadest view, there are two, man and nature, or labour and appropriate, natural agents.

Most persons, if not all, will yield a ready assent to the former when we say that all exertion, however slight, comes under its head, and it will hardly seem reasonable to object, that any commodities can be

*See Errata on back page

produced and consumed (for that must be included) without labour from the fact that man is only compelled to go and gather the store which the bounty of nature has or had, previously to man's existence, provided for his entertainment and sustenance.

Labour cannot be said to differ in kind, but only in degree, for both mind and body are essential to the labour of even the lowest animals, and it seems merely a question of the greater or less predominance given to each form in any particular act, which justifies us in calling it either bodily or mental.

To the motion of the lowest organism nervous force is essential, and brain is little else than nervous force, complicated by the evolution of the organism possessing it, and without bodily exertion no movement is perceptible, though it must be supposed to take place. The theories of philosophers cannot be regarded as produced without some movement of the brain, though we may not be able to perceive it. Such theories also as philosophers may by brain-labour work out are unknown to any but themselves, save when bodily labour has transferred them to the paper which is the medium of communication with the world. So that whether we consider the highest or lowest form of organism, both bodily and mental labour are necessary to produce any good result.

Using the word commodity altruistically,—that is,

as the thing relates to some one else,—it is clear that natural agents are essential to production, for however much mere labour may be a commodity to the individual, in respect of its providing him with such satisfaction as he may desire, yet in order that that satisfaction may be passed on to some one else, it is necessary that it should be embodied in some material form, for without that it cannot be called a commodity, and still less is it capable of being transferred.

Natural agents, just as labour, are capable of improvement, but they are still to be regarded as natural agents, for the sake of convenience in writing and speaking; and all machinery, mills, engines, and farms, are natural agents, which have been fertilized by the enterprise and genius of man.

Hereafter we propose to say something of the property which man is entitled to in the improvements of natural agents, for it is speedily becoming one of the most important economic topics in respect of the improvements effected by tenant-farmers in the natural agents, the possession of which has been by society conceded to others, namely, the landlords. It is only just and right that an improvement effected by one man on the land, as a natural agent belonging to another, should be returned to the former, or, that he should at any rate receive a compensation for the expenditure of his time, his money, or his wit, just in the same way as an inventor receives something in return for the benefits he confers on the natural agents, utilized by other labourers or employers of labour.

3. *Of the requisites for the continued increase of production.*—In speaking here of the increase of production, we do not merely mean the increase of production in proportion to the number of persons, but of its increase out of proportion to that number: of what is currently understood by the expression so misused by economists of the increase of wealth, or as we might say, to express it more fully, of the means adopted by man in order to increase the satisfactions of the community, so that notwithstanding the increase in the number of inhabitants, there may still be an increasing wealth among those persons.

Of the requisites to the continued increase of production there are three,—namely, Property, Exchange and Capital.

It will be regarded by many as extremely doubtful whether property is not merely a means of increase of production; but a positive requisite in consumptive-production for it is extremely hard,— nay, impossible to draw a line where we can say property begins or ends. Supposing man in a savage condition is his right of property only to commence when he has actually put his food into his mouth. Surely such an idea is too barbarous to contemplate.

Property seems as it were drawn out of mind, and projected over matter.

It is a subtle fiction or invention of the mind of man which, arising primarily in the conjunction of body and matter, when any man consumes that food which is essential to life is secondarily projected over the food which uncivilized man is apt to hoard for future consumption or to lay by for a rainy day, and is, thirdly, rendered more intensely material when it is imposed upon those natural agents which are not of themselves productive of satisfaction, but are endowed with reproductive energy by the labour and exertions of man.

Without any such subtle idea progress in wealth is impossible; wealth there may be but no progress, for in cases where saving is practically abolished by the denial of the right of man to those things which he has procured for human consumption, no human being would be so practically foolish as to save merely that others may, if they be stronger, deprive him of the results of his toil and labour.

The gradual progress of the idea of property is to be found well illustrated in Herbert Spencer's Sociology Chapter on Property, vol. ii., where it will be seen his investigations into the matter bear out our remarks upon its progress from the immaterial to the material, from the things as they are consumed to the things necessary for future production.

Property is a right conceded in order to induce labour and saving, that man may not be deterred from labour by the abstraction of any results he may thereby obtain and to continued increase of production may be regarded as the primary essential, for if property were recognized only in the things we actually consume no one would provide for a future consumption when his provision would be rendered useless and his labours nugatory by the abstraction of its results by the idle.

Of the second of the requisites to the continued increase of production, namely, exchange, there are two sorts, as is obvious,—namely, subjective and objective exchange.

By subjective exchange we mean the separation in the sorts of labour, or the transfer of each man to one particular service, which ultimately carries us on to the division of labour as generally understood, namely, the devotion of each individual not merely to the production of one commodity but to the production of one part of one commodity. By objective exchange we mean, as will no doubt require no explanation, the exchange of objects.

This second sort of exchange is the outcome of the former, for it is useless for two savages to agree to devote themselves to the making one of bows and the other of arrows, unless they consent after having done so to exchange the bows of the one for the egoistic equivalent in the arrows of the other.

From this slight explanation the reader will see that exchange, while founded upon property admitted among men in the necessaries for existence, is a power of great force in increasing the production of commodities. Perhaps no power is so great and all-pervading in Political Economy, because for the production of capital exchange is essential now, though of course it was not so formerly.

Property having been conceded by the consent of the individuals, exchange seems to follow as almost a matter of course, for hardly has man been allowed by consent to store up food for future use when he finds that greater rapidity in production is due to the greater continuity of labour, that the longer he continues his labour without interruption the quicker in proportion do its results accumulate; and having found this to be the case, it is but a small step to exchanging the superfluities which would soon result from such continuity of labour for the superfluities which he must see his companions are equally able to obtain by a similar continuity in their labour. Whether subjective exchange precedes objective exchange we can hardly tell, but probably objective exchange was originally the cause of subjective exchange. It is not, however, a matter of any great consequence which had precedence in order of time, for both are so important and so complimentary as to render any division as impossible as it is useless.

Of the third requisite for the continued increase

of production, namely, capital, we shall have much to say further on when we are considering the objective reproduction of wealth or the devotion of material agents to the reproduction of commodities.

A great deal of confusion of thought and ignorance is imported into Political Economy from writers being apparently quite in the dark concerning capital. Perhaps nothing has contributed so much to this confusion as the chapter in Mill's " Political Economy " on excess of supply, for such has been the reverence exhibited for the arguments there given that any true definition of capital has become impossible. Those arguments of Mill's are, it seems to us, the poorest part of his whole work, for they consist when closely examined of an endeavour to beg the question, and also of a *non sequitur* of the latter we have disposed. The endeavour to beg the question we hope later on to expose.

It would be misplacing our matter were we to explain fully the meaning of capital here, and all that is necessary is just to call attention to the obvious fact of its power of increasing the production of commodities. There is nothing else whose power is so fully recognized and so universally agreed to because of its extreme obviousness in any transaction of life.

Every merchant, trader, banker, and retailer—nay, every consumer throughout the length and breadth of the country knows the power of capital both as a consumer and producer, for capital enables us to consume as well as to produce; and as we hope to show capital originally was nothing but power of *future* consumption, which by exchange, either subjective or objective, became capable of being turned into present production, whereas capital, according to the objective economists, is something which *has been or is being* turned to present production.

The idea is one of far greater elasticity than is supposed, and means not so much what is useful as what is capable of utility, not the employment of the thing as economists will have it, but ability to employ the thing. As Professor Ruskin so truly remarks, it meant originally a store, a store capable of being rendered useful though not necessarily so used.

4. *Does nature contribute more to the efficacy of labour in some occupations than others?*—The question at the head of this section is one which has been cursorily treated and summarily dismissed by Mr. J. S. Mill; for his remarks see Book I, chapter i, sec. 3, of his " Principles of Political Economy."

Mr. Mill has, we think, treated the question very defectively, for from even his own point of view, namely, as a question of quantitive causation or simply as a question of the amount of each cause in any given effect, it is important, and treating it as we think it was intended to be treated, namely, from a compound quantitative view or as a question whether the amount of each cause is in two given effects different, it becomes a question of great importance to the wage-earning class.

It may be very unimportant to inquire whether in agriculture, for instance, man or nature contributes most to the result in the food when brought to market and sold, and no doubt many people will think it to be so. But few will consider it equally unimportant when we say that supposing, for the sake of argument, nature gives less effect in mercantile pursuits than in agricultural, therefore wages in mercantile pursuits are higher than in agricultural.

It is perfectly true that where both causes must contribute to a result we are justified in saying that they are equally important, but where there is a remuneration devoted to each cause it becomes important to note how much each cause contributes.

The question to regard Mill's simile is not whether 5 or 6 contribute most to 30, but whether in two sums of 30 A, who contributes 10 in one case and 20 in the other, is to get a larger or a smaller return in proportion to the amount he contributed in each case.

As a matter of fact it will be generally conceded that material agents contribute less to the result than labour.

It is only just and reasonable that he who contributes the greater quantity of cause in an effect should get the greatest results from his exertions, and this is undoubtedly the case in trade.

For instance, if a man in trade ventures on an innovation or invention by which he dispenses with some labour, he in reality transfers to himself part of the benefit which was expected in the payment for the commodity. Of the totality of causes, namely, abour and material agents, the amount of the cause, labour, is reduced, and by that reduction the inventor benefits.

The great difficulty in comparing trade and agriculture is, that people are apt to forget that all inventions have to be classed under the head of natural agents, just as improvements in land, so that discussing the question whether labour contributes more to the result in agriculture than trade, it would seem as if wages were lowest when labour contributes most to the result, namely, in agriculture. In fact, that the greater the compulsion man is under to labour the less is the reward he gets for his labour, or the more his works tend to become works of superogation the greater the result he obtains from them.

But so many points complicate the question as to render conclusions to some extent valueless, for density of population has of course a much more powerful influence than anything else; could we, however, estimate any one factor truly in any given case we should be conferring a great boon on economy.

Whatever thing man produces and is able to exchange procures a fixed result, and this result is divided between material agents (including capital under that head) on the one hand, and labour on the other, and the results of this struggle are always disastrous to the labourer in consequence of the increase of population and the consequent competition for it (the labour).

Labour is as constantly outrunning its power of subsistence as capital is constantly outrunning our power of reproductively consuming it.

CHAPTER II.

OF LABOUR.

1. *Of the different sorts of labour.*—There are few things which at first sight seem so easy to do and yet are, on second thoughts, so hard as to classify labour. It seems so easy to term it either bodily or mental, and then to point out which is which; but while we do this we shall find that there are some sorts of labour which seem to baffle all attempts at classification. The labour, for instance, of servants, singers, lecturers, and many other similar sorts of labour, seem to defy all our efforts to reduce them to order, and the more we try the more confused our ideas seem to become.

The following classification goes on the same lines as our divisions of wealth and value :—

$$\left.\begin{array}{l}\text{Bodily}\\\text{or}\\\text{Mental}\\\text{Labour}\end{array}\right\} \begin{array}{l}\text{subjective}\\\text{objective}\end{array} \begin{cases}\text{productive}\\\text{reproductive}\\\text{productive}\\\text{reproductive}\end{cases} \begin{cases}\text{egoistic}\\\text{altruistic.}\end{cases}$$

This classification will be found comprehensive, and will, moreover, show us how difficult it is to separate the sorts of labour in consequence of labour, which is subjectively reproductive being objectively productive, that is, in consequence of its being necessary to embody our desire in a material object if we wish them to produce a desire for the same thing in some one else.

Labour is regarded in this book either as creating satisfactions or as creating satisfactions embodied in material objects, and we must apologize for borrowing and altering the form of Mr. J. S. Mill's thunder.

Mr. Mill speaks of labour as creating utilities, a word which we venture to think is most highly objectionable on account simply of its ambiguity, and perhaps we may seem to have become by using a more general word more highly ambiguous; and yet, considering the definition which we have given to wealth, no other word seems permissible.

The word utility is objectionable because of nothing, in every case, may it be predicated that it is useful. That which is useful here and now is not useful there and then. Moreover, to define labour as producing utilities is simply to subject labour to the caprice of the writer, who may say, for instance, that the labour employed in producing gold watch-cases, sticks other than crutches, rings, trinkets, and such like articles, is not labour at all, that is in an economic sense.

The word satisfactions covers everything that man effectively demands, which is of course the primary object, and it also covers a vast multitude of things besides in such a way as to render all labour capable of being within the bounds of the definition. If labour produces a satisfaction for the individual who labours or for some one else, then it is capable of classification.

So comprehensive is this word that it will almost enable us to classify convict labour at the treadmill as producing satisfaction in a right-minded person by showing the force of justice to punish outrages on society. There is a certain amount of satisfaction in seeing wrong righted or the punishment of evil-doing, as is shown in the satisfaction produced by novel reading and play-going, few novels or plays being considered satisfactory where wrong is not righted and evil-doing punished.

The preference which we give to satisfactions over the word utilities is caused by its being a word relating exclusively to the present, whereas utility is a word which relates equally to the past and the future. A thing may be useful because it has or because it may become so; a thing cannot, however, be properly said to be satisfactory unless it actually is so at the present time; and as Political Economy deals with the present and not the future consumption, satisfactions is a better word.

2. *Of subjective labour subjectively regarded.*—This sort of labour should have been treated of in the Second Book under the head of subjective wealth,

but all things considered it is better here where labour is treated and discussed generally, because, as we have noted, that labour which is subjectively reproductive is objectively productive. Unless we see an object which labour has produced producing satisfaction, we cannot have transmitted to us a desire for the same kind of satisfaction.

Now, the primary division which we have given to labour is that labour which produces a sense of satisfaction in the individual who labours. Under this head comes all labour which man undertakes simply for his own amusement, such as boating, sailing, and amateur work of all kinds—work, that is, where the worker seeks for his remuneration in and for himself. Upon this sort of labour no remarks are necessary in an economical treatise. For, as we have mentioned before, altruistic satisfactions are the object of Political Economy.

Our second division of labour was that which produces a satisfaction for some one else merely, that is, in the labour, and of this sort is the labour of servants or musicians. The reward being commensurate to the trouble taken to produce satisfactions.

It is obvious to any one that it is only by giving altruistic satisfactions that we procure for ourselves any material reward, and consequently the bodily or mental labour undertaken to fit people for the situation they are about to fill in their station in life is simply subjectively productive of satisfaction in the individual. The labour of any lawyer, musician, teacher, or public servant previous to the rendering of the service, and which although not considered, or only considered when the question of reward arises, is purely egoistic, and can only come within practical economics when such labour is undertaken subject to an agreement such as an apprenticeship deed. This practical regard to the training of fit servants is falling into abeyance in a great measure, and the fact of the increasing disregard paid to such training is felt more and more by traders as their workman becomes more expensive to his master from a deficient ability to perform his services. It is customary, as we before mentioned, among most radical thinkers to regard all men as equal, and therefore equally able to perform all services, in fact to reduce mind to a uniform level, one might almost say of stupidity, and to cry down as restraints on man's freedom and a hindrance to trade all deeds of apprenticeship; but these kind of arguments, however pretty and theoretic, show an absolute inability on the part of the thinkers to consider facts—men are not equal, and no amount of argument will make them so.

The author had a discussion one day with a leading manufacturer of hats in London about apprenticeships in that trade in consequence of his (the author's) remarking on the deterioration in the manufacture of silk hats, and the trader attributed that deterioration to the increasing disregard of apprenticeships skilled, that is, sufficiently skilled workmen could not be obtained to perform the work and unskilful labour produces bad work.

Looking at the matter, however, from the view of an outsider, it seems to us that the cause of this deterioration may be traced partly to the manufacturers themselves, who are always so intent upon extending their markets as to disregard the profits good work will obtain, and also to an inability to compete successfully for trade, in consequence of the grinding of the powerful competition of the present day.

Subjectively reproductive labour is that sort of labour which produces the most immaterial satisfactions in material objects, that is to say, such labour as produces fancy goods, jewellery, and all the little fripperies of fashion. This sort of labour is labour in the transition period from the subjective to the objective form, and the more the goods become what Mill calls utilities, the more they cease to be subjectively reproductive, and the labour spent on them becomes* supply objectively productive; the less they influence the desire of other people the more they pass into the sphere of utilities or things which we cannot do without.

The labour which produces this class of articles is the most highly paid of any objectively productive labour, in all probability chiefly on account of its

*See Errata on back page

uncertainty of its doubly uncertain remuneration, first, in consequence of the perpetual change of fashion in articles of decoration, dress, &c., and, secondly, in consequence of the defalcations of purchasers.

The retail traders in these things, who of course are only the medium of payment between the producers and consumers, are in the habit of giving their customers long credit, and are in consequence often compelled to resort to law to enforce claims which are so old as to be resented by the consumers. Again these retail traders are also in some measure in their customers' hands, for those customers being the highest classes in society, it is considered not worth a retail trader's while to sue them for their unpaid bills, as so doing would give the trader a bad name in his own market, which of course is a great injury.

These causes which affect the retail trade must affect ultimately the wholesale one, for the retailers are a mere medium for passing the goods one way and their price another, and therefore these, among other causes, add to the profits of this sort of business on the ground simply of uncertainty of remuneration, than which nothing is a more fruitful source of profit.

3. *Of objective labour regarded objectively.*—This is the sort of labour which economists are so fond of

eulogizing as the labour *par excellence*. The labour which produces objects, particularly those objects which, as Mill says, embody utilities,—the idea is so simple as to require little illustration.

This labour is of two kinds, that which produces satisfactory objects, if we may be permitted the expression, and that which reproduces satisfactory objects, or things employed in producing satisfactory objects.

Of objectively productive labour there are as many kinds as processes in the manufacture and sale of any article of commerce from the production of raw material to its retail sale in the shops of a large city. In proportion to the division of labour or the number of processes through which any thing passes before it is consumed, so is the labour capable of being divided; to attempt, however, a division, or classification, seems impossible, for each article differs from its nature in the number of processes through which it passes.

It may, perhaps, be useful if we trace the various processes through which one or two common articles of commerce pass before they are consumed, so as to show the impossibility of further subdividing the sorts of labour.

Take, for instance, cotton cloth. The cotton has first to be grown, say in Surat or Carolina, which employs vast armies of workmen in planting and tilling it; then it has to be picked and afterwards packed in bales, also a matter of great labour, for subsequent transportation to the mill, at which it will ultimately be spun, and between its packing and spinning many people are engaged in squeezing a profit out of it; for not only is there the medium of conveyance such as railways, ships, and canals, but the grower probably sells to a broker, who possibly is engaged with his friends in getting up a corner in cottons, that is to say, buying in order that he may hold back till the price rises sufficiently for him to sell at a good profit to the spinner. Having got to the spinner, after giving all this benefit on its course, it passes on to the weaver, who gets another profit, then to the dyer, then to the merchant, then to the warehouseman, then to the retail trader, and, last but not least, to the consumer.

No one does business from pure philanthropy, and so all these persons have to be rewarded with a profit before the consumer gets any benefit or satisfaction from the proceeds.

Or to take an instance from bread. The wheat, we will suppose, is grown out west in America by one of those pioneers of civilization whose reward is hardly commensurate with the benefits they confer on society. The grain having been collected and stored is transported to a broker or merchant, say at Chicago, from whence it passes on to this country, yielding on its way a profit to the grower, the merchant, and the carrier. A corn factor having probably purchased it in London, to whom a profit is yielded, it passes into the hands, say, of the miller or distiller, according to its ultimate destination in food and drink, who both perform their duties upon it for a profit. Having left the miller's hands it gets to the baker, who ultimately renders it up to the consumer for a profit.

Looking at the matter in this light, it would seem as if almost the whole price of any article must be swallowed up in profit, but in proportion as the profit gets larger so the bulk dealt in gets still larger, and the profit is ultimately reduced to the very smallest dimension on every particular loaf. It is quite impossible to estimate exactly how much goes in profit and how much in mere labour of production, but it would probably be found, we think, that the ultimate profit of the baker would afford a very fair criterion of the matter, and if it really affords any guide at all, it shows how really small in proportion to price is the remuneration called profit that labour swallows, the greater proportion of the cost of any article.

Objectively reproductive labour is that labour which produces those things which are employed in production, such as the tools and implements of trade, the weaving and spinning machines, and other articles of a like nature.

There is nothing peculiar in this sort of labour or

any difference in production; it is merely an altruistically objective way of looking at things, or the view of the bearing of one thing upon another in the production of the latter.

A great deal of confusion of thought exists in Political Economy concerning labour which is reproductively employed. Mill, following Adam Smith, adduces as an instance of it labour employed in producing the subsistence of labourers, which is a very far-fetched idea, for why should the subsistence of bodily labourers be differentiated from the subsistence of mental labourers, such as doctors and lawyers, or the subsistence of the man of fashion, who is neither one nor the other, who is not a labourer at all save in a subjectively reproductive manner.

That which goes in the subsistence of objectively reproductive labour is capital or excess of supply. It is that portion of the products of the nation which has been produced in excess of the effective demand, and so it is devoted to the purchase of labour upon works which are, while in production, in excess of demand—that is, which can only be proved to be useful by being used objectively.

To explain more fully objectively, society may be divided into three classes—producers, consumers, and reproductive producers. Producers and consumers by exchange get an excess of supply, which excess is capable of being devoted to objectively reproductive labour; but because of its capability it does not follow that it will be entirely so devoted, in fact the probabilities are that it will not all be so devoted, a portion being used in augmenting consumption.

The wages of objectively reproductive labour may be said to come out of capital, but the wages of objectively productive labour cannot be said to do so under any circumstances, for capital cannot arise till after exchange; whereas the wages of objectively productive labour arise and are paid before any exchange takes or can possibly take place; so to consider them paid out of capital is to put the cart before the horse, and then to say that therefore the cart drives the horse.

The whole confusion to which this subject is given over may be traced back to Adam Smith, who, without fully understanding what is meant by capital, was yet so bold as to differentiate it into fixed and circulating, and to call food the latter and the instruments used in production the former. Capital is an idea incapable of being divided, because it is an idea whole and complete in itself. Who would be so foolish as to differentiate a seed into roots and branches? The seed is the idea as it is; not as it could or might become. The wages of objectively reproductive labour come out of capital, but because they come out of capital therefore they are not capital. Reproductive objects, such as spinning and weaving machines, railway stocks, 3 per cents., &c., &c., &c., come out of capital, and therefore they are not capital; they are the tree into which the seed, capital, has been transmuted. The seed is not the tree.

All this blundering in thought comes from not having clear and distinct ideas at the outset, from confusing object and subject, mind and matter, man and the things he consumes. The spinning jenny fetish of objective economists is the idol upon which their worship has been spent, and it has landed them in statements which are merely objects of ridicule to the believer in man and his aims.

This section is an endeavour to make the reader, looking at commodities or objects objectively, to point out that objectively labour may be classed into that which produces satisfying objects, or that which produces articles required in producing satisfying objects; therefore labour employed in producing satisfying objects, such, for instance, as the sustenance of labour, is simply objectively productive labour, and we should divorce from our minds the idea that it has any concern with capital at all.

4. *Of objective labour subjectively regarded.*—Nothing better illustrates the difficulty of classifying labour than the common division into agricultural, manufacturing, and commercial labour, and in conse-

quence of this being a subjective view of labour, it is of course a classification for objective economists to regard as useless and absurd.

Mr. Mill, then, at Book I, chap. ii, sec. 9, accordingly remarks that it subserves no useful purpose of classification; to him it would naturally not do so, for if you are regarding the matter objectively a subjective classification is not likely to be useful.

It seems that this classification rests upon the ideas of board, lodging, and the obtaining of those things. It is a rough and ready classification according to the services which the articles of commerce render, and nothing more shows the grandness of Hegel's philosophy or the development of all into one—the conjunction of mind and matter, for this is a material and mental classification at one and the same time; it is a material classification of articles based not upon the primary qualities inherent in them, but upon the secondary qualities which are inherent in mind, and it is so much used because of its comprehensiveness. It is a classification which takes in every thing from all points of view.

The objections which Mill finds to it is, of course, that some of the processes of objectively productive labour,—that is, labour which is employed during some of the processes of production, such as that of the miller,—is not agricultural labour; but looked at from the subjective view, it will of course be seen that the fact that a miller is a separate man from a farmer has nothing to do with the classification; the question simply is, what service does he render to man? There would be no difficulty whatever in the classification if commerce was abolished and every man satisfied his own necessities—if the farmer sowed, ploughed, manured, reaped, winnowed, ground, and baked by himself and for himself; but because all these are different processes therefore Mill must needs find fault with the classification. No classification that is of any use can be made upon the processes through which any consumable commodity passes, for each of the thousand and one passes through a different number and different sorts of process, and there would be not merely a classification of each article of commerce separately, but added thereto a classification of processes which would be endless.

There are then, as we have shown, three possible modes of classification and only three, and while the scientific economists will probably choose the two former the public will choose for use the last as being all-embracing.

5. *Of mental or bodily labour.*—Labour may be either bodily or mental,—that is, either more mental than bodily or *vice versâ;* for, as we have pointed out before, it must be bodily to some extent, and, as Mill says, it must be to some extent mental, for

no animal could perform properly the office of the stupidest hodman.

The tendency of modern times and one of the results of increasing wealth has undoubtedly been to make labour more mental and less and less bodily, though however much it tends in one direction it must certainly be both. The more immaterial agents become the greater is their power, and this is certainly true of man.

In this matter of labour, in which man is a combination of apposites, that man is most successful who most fully combines the two opposites in one product. Bodily labour is of all sorts the most sure and certain in getting its reward. As, however, more mind is introduced, the reward while becoming more uncertain, and in fact partly in consequence of the uncertainty, becomes in proportion greater; but there comes a time when mental power, too, far outstrips the bodily, and then no reward results. In no cases is this more perceptible than in those countries which have been wealthy, such as Italy and Spain. These countries are poor, and are likely to remain so, not for want of ability but from a plethora of it. Mind has outstripped matter, and man is anxious to get a reward for services which are not sufficiently material to be considered worth paying for. The Italian mind, perhaps, is noted for its intricacy and tortuousness—in a word, its power; but the Italians are a bodiless people, a people whose very activity of mind has rendered their bodies inert; too great a specialization of function has ruined the country. He who can be all things in all places is the successful man.

We are inclined to agree with Herbert Spencer that the system of compulsory education, as it is called, is exerting just the very opposite influence which was intended. It is stamping out mind by a compulsory production of equality. It degrades the reasoning powers by an increase in the faculty of memory or receptivity; man becomes under its influence a machine for holding, not as he should become a machine for grinding; the memory is stuffed with facts such as can produced successfully at a competitive examination, and is rendered incapable of reasoning and generalizing.

For this reason, however, we differ from Herbert Spencer in regarding this compulsory education as a good thing, for it represses a too great mental exertion; while it does not hinder bodily work, it has a tendency to prevent such an exertion of the mind as will cause man to be idle and lazy of body. As we said before, to be seated in the mean is the sure basis of success, and too powerful a mind is undoubtedly productive of a lazy body; though it is quite true that the opposite—that is, a want of mind—is also productive of idleness, the difficulty being to predicate which is the cause in any given case, most persons infallibly turning to the latter as is currently called. Nothing is more easily explained.

By inequality, or differentiation, or specialization, call it which you will, and whether it be subjective or objective, proceeds the great increase in wealth, power, and prosperity. It is a fact well brought out by Adam Smith, that the greater the specialization of labour the greater is the objective result in commodities. In the first chapter of his " Inquiry into the Causes of the Wealth of Nations," Adam Smith writes :—" I have seen a small manufactory of this kind (pins) where only ten men were employed, and where consequently some of them performed two or three distinct operations. But though they were very poor and therefore but indifferently accommodated with the necessary machinery, they could, when they exerted themselves, make among them about twelve pounds of pins in a day. There are in a pound of pins upwards of 4000 pins of a middling size. Those ten persons, therefore, could make among them upwards of 48,000 pins in a day. Each person therefore making a tenth part of 48,000 might be considered as making 4800 pins in a day. But if they had all wrought separately and independently, and without any of them having been educated to this particular business, they certainly could not each of them have made 20, perhaps not one pin in a day,—that is, certainly not the 240th, perhaps not the 4800th, part of what they are at present capable of performing in consequence of a proper division and combination of their different operations."

There is nothing so powerful in increasing the quantity of commodities produced for man's gratification as this differentiation of labour, a differentiation which operates in a similar way to the differentiation of consumption, though, in consequence of the power of exchange and man's propensity to save, the results of the differentiation of labour exceed the increase of consumption.

It is the business of any progressive and successful manufacturer or man of business to take advantage of this division so as to get for himself more profit from his labour. Even lawyers, bankers, and, in fact, every sort of labour, is capable of being to some extent reduced by specialization, and high specialization of work is a mark of high power of producing any commodity. This specialization is not, however, an unmixed benefit to the race of man, as it renders man incapable of action out of a still more limited sphere. Those who regard the object produced as all-important naturally regard the division of labour as an unmixed benefit; but while it renders the rich richer it renders the poor more incapable of becoming rich, for by reducing the variety in their work it renders their minds more inert.

Perhaps the most noticeable effect of the increasing division of labour is that which Adam Smith called attention as the third of the effects it produces, namely, the increasing ability to employ machinery; the man whose labours are reduced to the smallest possible compass is not only more easily able to apply machinery to his branch of labour, but is also more ready to see how the machinery may be improved, and in doing so perhaps is able to introduce a further division and reduction of labour, so ultimately increasing the product in goods from the same amount of labour. This reduction, it need hardly be pointed out, goes to benefit the employer of labour alone and correspondingly injures the workman, for not only is the limited demand of consumers supplied with less labour, but the workmen's wages are correspondingly reduced in consequence of the increasing uniformity of his labour and the decreasing quantity of brains required to perform his task. As we noted in the preceding section, remuneration is in proportion to the brain power materially expressed.

This reduction, however, has its bright side, for it enables a greater variety of objects to be consumed, and in that way the labour is again increased; but this trespasses on our succeeding section.

7. *Of the effects upon labour or wages of protection.*— One of the objects at which protection aims is to prevent the too great diminution of labour in conse-

quence of its division. In a word, it is a means of keeping up the wages of labour.

Taking any country, it will be found that by far the greater majority of the population are sustained by labour alone; they have no means of subsistence other than what is afforded by their labour. It follows from this that any great reduction of labour is simply an abstraction of the means of subsistence of a corresponding portion of the population, or, we should say, perhaps not an abstraction of means of subsistence from some, but a diminution in the degree of comfort in subsistence of all the labourers in the nation.

Now it stands to reason from this that anything which tends to raise wages goes in benefiting the majority of the population, for upon that they subsist. We might perhaps be considered to beg the question did we refer to what we have said before of the source from which the wages of objectively productive labour are drawn, namely, the consumption of commodities, that the wages of this form of labour come from the commodities produced and consumed; we will, therefore, as it were, argue the matter backwards.

In any given country during any given period there is a fixed limit to the quantity of any commodities effectively demanded. I use one pin to my tie, and what is true of this is true of all things consumed, namely, that there is a limit to the number or quantity of the things used. Nothing will make me use two pins or two hundred. I have an object, and when that object is satisfied anything beyond is excess.

This being the case, suppose a country under protection is producing two commodities, the production of one of which would be extinguished if the protection were withdrawn, as the production of that commodity would be transferred to another country.

Withdraw the protection, and the country in question has to satisfy its needs from one manufacture by exchange for that which the other country now produces.

The effect of the division of labour would, in the given commodity here, exert its full force, and the limited quantity desired for home consumption would be produced with the smallest quantity of labour. Home consumers, however, still want the other commodity, and in order therefore to get it more of the home commodity must be produced for exchange ; but assuming for a moment a doubled production, the sum of the labour would be reduced and the same number of labourers would be clamouring for it. If 24,000 pins, to go to Adam Smith's simile, require the labour of, say, seven men to produce them, 48,000 pins would only take say ten men to produce them in a day. The other commodity is now being produced in a foreign country, and to get it we must resort to exchange, with what result ? In the first place, all the foreign effective demand is satisfied as we have seen, and so we are offering them goods which they don't want to purchase for those which we do want. Inasmuch then as all exchange depends upon the wants of the parties exchanging, we are going to market with something which has a diminishing demand, and our profit will probably be changed into a loss. We are giving what no one wants, to obtain something which we want very badly, and the result is no excess of supply to us, no profit. It becomes like a bankrupt sale; our goods are forced down the throat of people who don't care about them, and so give us very little for what we give them. Our labour therefore gets badly paid for the home commodity, and our objectively reproductive labour suffers from a want of capital wherewith to keep it at work. The home produced commodity in consequence of the division of labour gives the smallest possible return to labour in wages, and the foreign produced commodity is bought at a loss. The country, its protection being withdrawn, goes to market with a depreciated currency in goods. For the currency or purchase power of commodities lies in the wants of the other person with whom we are doing business. Labour is under Free Trade forced into the least labour remunerative channels, and vendors go to market with a depreciated currency involving them in a loss of profit.

The question, however, turns in a great measure

upon the extra supply of the home commodity produced. If, say, for every 20 per cent. of production taken away from the now foreign produced commodity we get a 25 per cent. extra consumption of the home commodity, then of course no one suffers any loss, neither labourers nor merchants, except perhaps those whose capital being invested in a ruined business is rendered valueless, and so are unable to turn it into the other remunerative channel.

Wise legislation then should seek always to import into the country new sorts of labour, for the greater the number of commodities a country produce the greater in proportion is the amount of wage producing labour, and the greater value do the goods bear in exchange when sold, and so the greater is the quantity of capital produced. We may sum this argument up by the following general statement of it. Every reduction of price involves a reduction of labour, and assuming (which one is not generally justified in doing) an expenditure equivalent to the reduction of price, the sum of the wage producing labour is lessened; consequently, unless for every 20 per cent. less cost 25 per cent. extra consumption be proved to exist, Free Trade must injure the country which seeks for it.

There are a certain class of economists who in the face of an excess of imports over exports of upwards of £200,000,000, have yet the impudence—for such is all we can call it—to say that imports pay for exports, and you cannot consequently import more than you can export, and deduce many highly incorrect conclusions from a complete blindness to facts as they exist. When we come to deal with money, we shall point out that the object of money is to measure not the commodity (save in small and petty transactions), but the man's desire for it. That when I go to deal with a merchant I am considering whether what I am giving up is equivalent not to the thing bought, but to my or someone else's desire for it; consequently this astonishing excess of imports over exports shows that that is the measure of our desire for the commodities of other persons, in excess of their desire for our commodities. However much home exchanges may enable us at present to support such an expenditure, a time must come when they will cease to do so. It is a sign of diminution in objectively reproductive employment in England. The capital the turnover of the country is producing is being used to pay for things we want and can't produce, and consequently what some people choose to call the wages fund is being distributed in places other than this country.

Objectively exchanges may be said to balance; we give one material object and get in return another material object.

Subjectively exchanges never do balance; we give one more or less valuable thing, and get one less or more valuable thing.

If in the first case I give an old hat and get a gold watch, here exchanges balance; one material object is given and one material object is got, and no profit or loss can result—so says objective economy; to which subjective economy would reply, that is perfectly true, and its truth is such as to show its polemical inutility as an argument; exchange, it is true is objectively balanced, but subjectively I who gave the old hat have made a vast profit on the transaction; the supply has exceeded in amount the effective demand of my old hat, and I say so upon the authority of some other person, a third person who is no party to the exchange, but who tells me that he would have given more for the gold watch than I have given, or what he considers my old hat to be worth in exchange. This explains the trifling difference between subjective and objective economy. The latter in effect always begs the question, for the writers say that wealth means those things which are capable of satisfying our desire, and then having asserted that exchanges balance they beg the question of the amount of desire by inferring its equality in exchange.

We merely wish to state here our views, and why we consider Free Trade arguments a gross imposition. Whether we regard them from the labourer's point of view, or whether we regard it from the merchant's point of view, the fact remains from the subjective view that unless protection is useless, as it may possibly be conceived to be, Free Trade must injure the country.

8. *Of the limit of labour.*—The limit of all labour is the limit of effective demand for commodities, a statement so obvious, that were it not for the amusing theories of labour being limited by capital in some mysterious manner, which 'have been propounded by economists, it would require no illustration.

Of the commodities which we effectively demand, there are two sorts, namely, those demanded for productive consumption—that is, the consumption which gives us a sense of satisfaction—and those demanded for objectively reproductive consumption ; that is, the demand for the tools and implements which are employed in producing commodities, and by the quantity of these demands labour must be limited.

One would have supposed that the words effective demand showed us, as clearly as they could, the limit of labour, for when a man effectively demands any thing, he must have worked to get it. It may be objected to this that many persons who do no work effectively demand a great many things. A has a store of goods, part of which he gives to B to induce him to work and obtain some other commodity. It will be said B is being employed out of A's store or capital, and therefore his labour is limited by A's the cause, and endeavouring to eradicate it with the birch. The art of life is to be and not to be above your work.

In the present day this country suffers from a too small quantity of labour—a too powerful centralization of it. The unemployed are vast in numbers, the over-employed are being increasingly killed off. The country would undoubtedly benefit could the work be more distributed, could the protection of labour be more rigidly enforced. The question may well be asked, will the individual sacrifice his likes and dislikes to the good of the community—can we produce greater equality of mind? Compulsory education seems to have in a measure answered the question; it is a communistic device for producing equality of mind.

Mind, like everything else, is limited in its power in any individual, and as we see in the current caricatures of the day its increase involves a diminution of body. It is in consequence of this limitation that greater retentiveness of memory is a diminution of the power of reasoning, specializing in one direction is a diminution of our power in another; if the power of the mind of any given individual was unlimited, then of course this would not be true.

6. *Of the differentiation of labour.*—Perhaps nothing is so well known and understood as the theory of the differentiation, or division of labour, as it

capital, but this is not the usual case; as a rule A and B are merely exchanging labours. A may or may not have a store; if he has, then it is true to say he has supported labour from capital, but a very small quantity of labour is really so supported.

In the case of an isolated individual it stands to reason that his effective demand for productive consumption is the primary cause and support of his labour. His desire for food sets him to work to get it, and its result remunerates his labour; having satisfied that demand for productive consumption for a time, he may then, if he choose, devote a portion of his spare time to producing say a spade or other thing useful for reproductive consumption. It does not, however, follow that he will do so.

Under the altruistic view, caused by exchange, the process is not in the least altered in total quantity though it is in individual quantity. A and B, two labourers, engage to devote themselves each to the production of one commodity only and then to exchange. Here the result of A's labour remunerates B's labour. The effective demand for productive consumption of the two put together is so far the limit of the total quantity of labour; but it may be that although A's labour employs B's labour, yet that the quantity of the former given for the latter is less than the latter, still the effective demand for productive consumption has been the limit of the total quantity of labour, though it has not limited the precise quantity each one does. The matter, then, so far is clear. Labour employs labour, and capital does not in this case, or in the majority of cases, employ or limit the labour in any way.

But carrying on the case further, we see that A may have produced more of his commodity than B in the same time, so that when the exchange takes place A may still have some remaining. It is then supposable that A may say to a third person, C, if you will do me a service or produce some given thing, then I will give you part of what remained over after the above exchange, and C's labour would in this case be supported out of capital. Still it would not be true to say that C's labour was limited by capital, unless by so doing you merely mean that A could not employ C longer than his store lasted. It may only require a portion of A's capital or store to remunerate C for his labour, and therefore it can only be predicated of C's labour that it is limited by the effective demand of the community for reproductive consumption; or if what C produces be for productive consumption then it is still limited by the effective demand, though not then for reproductive consumption.

Effective demand therefore is the limit of labour.

Capital, however, limits the labour in a way different to that usually meant by economists; it enables us to import more effective tools into production. Suppose, now, in the above case C had produced for A a spade, a plough, or a steam-engine. A would when he set to work again perform his allotted task with less labour. It would be very little use his continually labouring for the same time, for he would produce a great deal more than B in that time, and he would find no effective demand perhaps for that excess, so that his capital would here have limited his labour, that is to say, would have reduced it, and in this sense capital limits labour.

Further complications than those above supposed cannot be brought into the discussion to prove that capital limits labour, or any paradoxical proposition of that sort. Capital, as we shall see hereafter, depends for its limitation more on ignorance of the amount of effective demand than anything else, and the question how much we spend on labour depends upon a hundred and one causes, such as invention, fashion, new desires, &c.

CHAPTER III.

OF MATERIAL AGENTS.

1. *Of the different sorts of material agents.*—To endeavour to classify material agents seems almost an impossibility; that is to say, to attempt any such classification objectively; for we should have to begin with a spade and end with a hundred-ton gun, or begin with a pin and end with a calculating machine.

Material agents can only be said to differ in respect of their immateriality or force; the greater the immateriality or productive force of any agent the greater is the result materially.

The best known of agents is the earth, an agent whose force is so bound up in it that it produces spontaneously many of the good things we consume. Man, however, by irrigation, manure, and other means, is enabled to give to the soil a greater productive effect.

Material agents and labour act in an inverse ratio; that is to say, the more productive the material agent becomes, the less labour is required to produce any given result. Naturally it will occur to many that this is merely the reverse view of the theory of the differentiation of labour; it is simply regarding the matter from the point of view of the object instead of the subject or man the labourer. It is, however, of great importance to man that material agents should be improved, that farms should be made more productive, that spinning and weaving machines should tend to produce a greater quantity in a given time; but it must always be borne in mind that improvements, however good, may be injurious to man's well being. Production may become so excessive in consequence of improvement that the balance of desire in exchange is on the wrong side and no profit results. Paralysis of labour ensues, for if producers are compelled to sell they are sure to lose, and they are then unable to employ labour in producing further supplies.

It might possibly be a good thing for trade if some check could occasionally be placed upon invention and the improvements of material agents generally, but at the same time it must be confessed that to calculate when was a fit time to impose such a restriction would be nearly impossible. It would moreover tend greatly to prevent the labours of inventors, who, seeing the doubts of their inventions being utilized by others, and the doubtfulness in consequence of any return, would be proportionately inert in considering the possibilities of improvement.

To attempt any objective classification of material

agents seems not only impossible, but useless. Subjectively, however, that is in respect of the source from which their power is derived, a division may be made. There are, then, two sources from which they derive their power : man and nature, and while the productive stimulation which man's inventive genius affords is obvious, we cannot but admit that within certain limits the increase of natural force is a decrease of productiveness, that is to say, it tends to render man apathetic and sluggish, and so to decrease the ultimate product in commodities. But we propose to consider these points in another section.

2. *Does material productiveness naturally produced favour production?*—Perhaps no part of the science of economy supplies us with a better test of the subjectivity or objectivity of the science than the answer which we regret to say must be given to this question.

It is a deplorable fact that the more nature does for man the less man is disposed to do for himself, and nothing tends so much to idleness as the ease of the surrounding circumstances under which it is man's lot to be cast. Nothing also so well illustrates the idea which Mr. Doubleday took such pains to prove—we mean the idea that nature is perpetually struggling with the external condition ; and, within certain limits, the more wretched man's condition, the more chance there is of his improving it. We say within certain limits, for there are cases such as Greenland, Norway and Siberia, where the conditions of life are so hard as to render man's efforts almost futile.

Professor Hearn writes: "Experience has indeed shown that natural advantages, like the advantages of fortune, do not always bring to their possessors the full benefit that might be derived from them." It seems to us that however much this state of things is to be deplored, yet it becomes the business of man, by means of government, to obviate it, and seeing that the state of things is paradoxical, it is not too much to say that the remedy may seem equally at variance with vulgar logic.

Search the world round and you cannot fail to see that in such countries as India, Italy, Greece, Spain, and the middle parts of America the very fertility of the soil is destructive of the energy and enterprise of man. The greater the fertility of matter the greater the sterility of mind. As this is acknowledged to be so by most thoughtful persons, does it not seem to follow that it is the duty of government to render nature sterile in effect in order that fertility of mind may result? That the more production is restrained the greater will the result be on man in stirring him up to obtain that which ease causes him to cease from desiring. Locke, upon the principles of mind which he advocated and so clearly elucidated, would have been undoubtedly a protectionist.

The question how such a thing can be done must naturally depend upon the form which the productiveness of the locality takes. Labour must be forced into the most subjectively productive, and therefore into the most objectively unproductive channels. To stifle production would be absurd, but in those countries where the bounties of nature are the greatest the stronger should be the force of the protection.

It may, however, be said that the prostrating cause is the heat which man is unable to fight against, and that before any such measure should be taken, provision should be made for getting rid of the heat. The capabilities of adaption of the human frame seem naturally to obviate this objection. The type of man will change, and with the type the form. From an idle, lazy and *insouciant* type of being, whose only idea is the sufficiency of the moment, will spring a type not only of superior mental development, but of more powerful bodily form. The productiveness of the country has been the ruin of the peoples, that is, from our view of prosperity.

To objective economists natural productiveness must favour production, and those countries which nature most favours must be the richest. Where the soil produces more, more must be produced, and to suppose Spain poor is absurd. Spain is one of the richest countries in the world naturally, not merely in agriculture but in minerals also, and it is perhaps odd that people who don't understand economy should try to make out its poverty.

Protection in Spain is in a great measure abortive, because misapplied. It seems that the great object in Spain is to keep goods out, and not, as it should be, to compel interior production. It is no use keeping goods out simply, for the inhabitants would naturally cease to use the things they could not get; it does not therefore follow that they would continue to labour at home to obtain them. The object of protection is to force labour into the more subjectively productive channels.

3. *Does material productiveness mentally produced favour production?*—As the converse of the preceding proposition, it seems naturally to follow that the answer to the above question must be in the affirmative; a fact which conclusively shows that God's ways are not as man's ways. The very lavishness of nature being a retardation of man's progress, seems conclusive proof that man's progress is, or should be, the object in Political Economy, and not simply material productiveness or unproductiveness, for the more material the productiveness, unless caused by man, the more rapidly he slides into prehistoric barbarism.

It is to material productiveness mentally caused that England owes her present power and wealth, and it is to the very same cause that America owes the rapid and gigantic strides she is making in the struggle of life. All this progress is caused by the friction of mind by the perception and acknowledgment of inferiority which is the motive power in competition. In a word, we come round to Locke's idea that the greater good moves not the will but uneasiness. All invention is due to that cause. Perhaps the most notable instance of it was the production of the spinning jenny by Arkwright; the picture of Arkwright and his wife are well known, and show conclusively the uneasiness which supplied the motive power.

Arkwright saw and felt the intense strain and exertion which his wife suffered in spinning and the small result produced, and it is to that perception that the invention was due. Hardly had the invention been in practical use when other men were stirred up to find means for improving. What, it may be asked, was their motive power; was it not uneasiness consequent upon the perception of Arkwright's success, a sort of jealousy inherent in human nature and caused in most cases by uneasy circumstances? Here you see the original start, instead of producing more idleness in consequence of the greater ease with which the commodities are obtained, has actually produced just the very opposite. The more man goes on inventing, that is, giving increased power to the material agents of production, the more he is stirred up to fresh exertions.

To take a more modern case, when oil lamps had superseded the older methods of lighting the streets, man did not cease to desire more light. The extra light obtained by the oil was, as it were, the cause of the invention of gas, and gas has been but a motive power in favour of electric lighting. And what is the reason?

Man always seeks to get the most result with the least labour, and as every man by invention gets rid of some labour, so he is enabled to draw to himself the benefit which accrue the reward which is reserved for the greater increase of commodities, with a decrease of the exertion which is required to produce them.

It will not unnaturally follow that Free Trade in inventions is as great a good as Protection is in securing progress under the enervating influence of natural productiveness. But by Free Trade in inventions, we mean of course perfect freedom to sell the results of man's brain-work; the abolition of the Patent Laws would merely lend to the confiscation of property. Property in the results of brain labour is just as defensible from an economic point of view, as it is in the results of bodily labour, and by Free Trade no one can mean the abolition of property of whatever kind for trade only exists in property.

4. *Objectively the efficiency of material agents is increased by facility of conjunction.*—Having pointed out in the preface that the ideas, wealth and value, are ideas of the conjunction of mind and matter, that is to say, of consumptive production, it would seem to follow from this that the nearer to the consumers the producers are, the greater will be the production.

As has been pointed out by Adam Smith, facility of communication, that is, conjunction, tends to increase objective wealth. As the difficulties of transport are overcome by better roads, improved ships, and the building of canals and railways, so motives are held out to producers to produce and exchange more than they have hitherto done.

The enormous profit obtained by the Duke of Bridgwater's family from the building of the famous canal which bears his name, is proof of the great service which he thereby rendered to trade, and in a similar way we may gauge the result of George Stephenson's exertions in the production of railways; no one, perhaps, has exercised so potent an influence in the material development of the wealth of the world as George Stephenson.

Different countries are differently affected by these means, their natural conditions being different. In hilly countries, such for instance as Norway and Switzerland, the difficulty of communication is naturally increased, and may be rendered of such force as to cause quite a stagnation of prosperity. Where everything has to be carried up and down hill, railways become but little better as a means of transport than canals, and man himself is reduced to a beast of burden.

In flat countries, such as Holland and China, we see that the very flatness has contributed by means of canals to wealth; those goods are produced which, had the inhabitants been compelled to distribute by means of themselves on land carriage, would never have been produced at all. Greater facility of obtaining in cases where that greater facility conduces to labour must ultimately conduce to the wealth or well-being of the country, and the rewards given to the improvers of communication are proof positive of its being the case.

Countries, however, differ very much in the facilities of water-carriage which nature has provided. In England the facilities which nature afforded are not very great. But sufficient has been done by nature to enable man to contribute considerably to the result. America owes much of its prosperity to the efficient water-carriage which nature has provided. It may be that to the mountainous character of Spain its poverty is in a great measure due. The great rivers of Spain are separated from one another by intervening mountains, and commerce between two valleys is consequently restricted.

It has always been noticed in confirmation of this view that the first settlers in any country settle according to the facilities of water-carriage; they swarm first up the rivers before settling inland, and penetration into the interior is due to the following out of the river branches.

5. *Subjectively the efficiency of material agents depends upon difficulty of conjunction.*—We must again call attention to the economic meaning of the word difficulty. Difficulty is equivalent economically to remunerative labour, and therefore when we say that the efficiency of material agents depends upon difficulty of communication, we mean that in those cases where no strain is put upon man's power or exertion ease of obtaining by means of easy communication does not increase wealth. When the force necessary to overcome the obstacle is not supplied by man there is no increase in wealth. It is to this that the outcry against private property in land and capital is due.

Suppose, for a moment, that all the internal traffic of any country was carried on by means of road traffic with horses and oxen, then the mere facilitation of consumption of that same quantity of commodities would be no increase in wealth. Every consumer would still remain just as much but no more a consumer than before, and therefore no more wealthy, for consumption is wealth.

The facilitation of carriage of the goods would, however, throw a certain quantity of labour out of the market, and the labourers would to that extent be injured, for their consumption would partly be transferred to their richer neighbours.

But, supposing that the facilitation of communication was to cause, as it might very well do, an increase in the amount of labour, then no one is injured, the power of consumption is restored to the labourers and increased in the other consumers.

If, on the introduction of the railways, greater difficulty of communication had not arisen in consequence of the railways having been productive of more labour than the original coach and waggon system, then there would have been less wealth in the country, less power of consumption. The increase of consumption consequent upon facilitated communication was such that the reduction of the labour engaged in production was more than counterbalanced by its increase. In a word, subjectively there was more difficulty in consuming.

Supposing it requires a force on my part amounting to x to enable me to lift a pound weight, which operation we will call wealth, and some one were to invent a method by which I could still lift the pound weight by only exerting $\frac{1}{2} x$, then subjectively there is less wealth, although objectively, or as regards the pound weight, the wealth remains the same. Now, supposing it followed that, notwithstanding the reduction of exertion, I still continued to exert the force x and so lifted two pounds, then wealth would be increased. The same subjective operation produces a greater objective result. Still subjectively wealth remains stationary, and it would only be on exerting a greater force than x that wealth would be really increased.

This principle is the principle upon which all arguments concerning the increase of wealth must turn, for, unlike the example given above, in wealth the force dominates the weight, that is, the weight, to continue the simile, can only be increased by means of the force exerted, and it is upon this ground that the argument is subjectively true that greater difficulty of communication is greater wealth.

As we said in the preface, what is saved is wasted, and what is spent is gained.

The objective argument is easy to understand, it is only the subjective one which is difficult, and therefore fails to commend itself to the vulgar mind. The subjective method or idea is in this system considered as the dominator of the objective view, and from this the conclusion may be drawn that ease of production is not, as is supposed by objectivists, conducive to wealth unless that greater ease is productive of greater difficulty; consequently from the subjective view the Free Trade argument having begged the question propounds a *non sequitur;* having asserted simply that reels of cotton are wealth, it becomes a *non sequitur* to say that wealth is increased by their being procured cheaper under Free Trade; subjectively cheaper procurement is no increase in wealth unless greater consumption results from such cheapness. The reduction of price of a daily paper from 2d to 1d is no increase in the wealth represented thereby unless the circulation is thereupon more than doubled.

6. *Some considerations concerning the opposition of the working classes to material agents.*—The reasons which operate upon the working classes, in such a way as to render them hostile to the introduction of better and improved material agents, have been noticed in the preceding section. They are reasons the subjectivity of which seems to render them outside the discussions of ordinary economists; but the potency of which cannot be too fully dwelt upon. They are the great motor powers in Socialism.

It is essential to the increase of the prosperity of any country that the number of persons employed in labour should be constantly on the increase; unless this is so, poverty must ultimately result; for their decrease only decreases the consumption of the country, while it increases that of the rich to a certain extent. A portion of consumption is abstracted from the poor, and a portion is of course added to the rich. Now there are two means by which we are enabled to consume, capital and labour, and whereas every consumption by capital tends to reduce the objective wealth, every consumption by means of labour tends to produce objective wealth. The false supposition upon which economists are too fond of enlarging is, the supposition that the supposed extra capital which is consequent upon the reduction of labour, goes to employ labour, that in fact it is directly returned to the poor; but this is not so, a good deal of it is consumed by the possessors of capital, capital attracting capital and being directly consumed by the rich; whereas the part that returns to the poor is limited by the reproductive demand of the moment which may be great, or it may be small—there may be a great railway to build or a canal to make, or there may not; but it does not follow that there will be reproductive employment commensurate with the increased capital.

The arguments of objective economists, like Mill, on this point grind round in an everlasting circle. Less labour is employed on unproductive consumption, but the result is more capital; capital employs labour, therefore there is still the same quantity of labour. To argue like this is to show that there is always the same quantity of labour in the world neither more nor less, and that economy is a mill which takes a patch of labour from unproductive consumption and puts it on to productive consumption, so that no one is benefited or injured, but perhaps we wrong them, and the idea is that for every one labourer taken from what they term unproductive consumption, one and a half are employed reproductively. The argument, however, still has the eternal grind about it which is so erroneous.

The whole question turns upon the limit of labour. Mill says, like most economists, that labour is eternal, or has no assignable limit. He writes at Book I, chapter 5, sec. 3:—" While on the one hand industry is limited by capital, so on the other every increase of capital gives, or is capable of giving, additional employment to industry, and this without assignable limit;" but a little further down he writes, " If Government employed all the labour it could exact productive labour from all to whom it allowed a share of food, and there would be no danger of labour falling short, so long as there was a want unsatisfied."

It is needless almost to point out that these two statements are entirely contradictory, the former being objective, the latter subjective; therefore the latter governs the former, and capital will not give employment to industry without assignable limit, because effective demand is always falling short, and sometimes does so to such an extent that a mere reduction of the amount of the return on the interest will not compel its employment.

The reason then which acts so forcibly on the labouring classes in stirring them up to oppose improvement, is their inability to forsee the amount of the extra consumption which will be produced by reason of the reduction of labour in any present production. They know better than most that the amount of profit which the capitalist obtains by reducing the labour necessary to produce a fixed quantity of goods, will not necessarily be spent by him productively, that it is possible for him to employ it in such a manner as to still further reduce the labour, notwithstanding that it does not at present employ labour. Moreover, as a general rule, the amount of labour which each additional quantity of capital is enabled (as objective economists say) to employ, is less than the amount which the same preceding quantity of capital employed. Or, to put it concretely, so as to explain if £100 employs one man then £200 will not employ two men but something less than two, say a man and a boy, and £300 will only employ two men and so on; so that from a labourer's point of view and from the Government point of view too, the country is not benefited to the eternal extent supposed by Mr. Mill, though of course there is a benefit.

But in the interest of the country it must be impressed upon the labouring classes that, however false the eternity arguments of objective economists may be, eternity arguments are equally false when brought forward by them—the labourers. There is a point beyond which the labour cannot be reduced; we shall never arrive at a time when the touching of a spring by one man will produce for every man who possesses a part of the machinery, and that although at times the causes above pointed out do operate very hardly on the poor, yet they are generally benefited in the end, the excessive reduction of labour consequent upon the improvements in material agents must stop, and then the capitalists are really no better off than before, for their interests and profits are reduced and the sum of the labour increased.

We cannot, however, resist the temptation to further expose Mill's arguments on this point. He writes as follows :—Suppose the capitalist and landowner laid by surplus profits, and unproductive expenditure reduced to its lowest limit, and consequently there are no longer customers for the goods formerly produced, the goods it is said will remain unsold, *but this is seeing only one half of the matter*. In the case supposed, there would be no longer any demand for luxuries on the part of the capitalist and landowner, but when those classes turn their income into capital they do not thereby annihilate their power of consumption, they do but transfer it to the labourers to whom they give employment. Now there are two suppositions in regard to labourers, either there is or is not an increase of their numbers proportional to the increase of capital. If there is, there is no difficulty; if there is not, then the labourer becomes a consumer of luxuries, and the capital employed in producing luxuries is still so employed, but the luxuries instead of going to the few go to the many."

Now, in the first place, let us ask how can a man cease to consume and yet continue to do so ? If I cease to eat caviare, am I compelled to use a steam hammer ? Unless I am it becomes absurd to say that a cessation of unproductive consumption by the rich will produce productive consumption among the poor, which is what Mill's first argument amounts to. He says the unproductive consumption of the rich, by being put an end to, transfers the things consumed to the poor. That because A ceases to demand, therefore B must do so; all this sort of argument arises from blindness to the fact that effective demand limits the labour and not capital, and that if one class ceases to consume the other must cease to produce, and there will be no capital whatever to transfer.

But the most amusing part of the argument is the finale, which tells us that if there is an increase of labourers proportional to the supposed increase of capital the case presents no difficulty. We should have thought it presented the very obvious difficulty that the poor are not benefited and the rich are injured, a very gratifying result truly. Look, however, at the alternative result which, by supposing a diminishing population, is to benefit one class at the expense of the other,—truly a good method for increasing progress.

It is obvious that we may retort upon Mill: this is seeing only one half of the question. His consumers are divided into two classes, rich and poor; those of our readers who have understood the theory of the differentiation of consumption will see at a glance that supposing the effective demand of the rich to be transferred to the poor, there will still be less labour for the poor to get a living by, for the poor will not give so much to obtain the extra available quantity of commodities as the rich did, so that unless the consumptive power expended by the poor can be proved to be greater than that which was taken from the rich, injury must result. Therefore Mill's arguments prove either a positive or a possible diminution of labour and wealth.

There are too many writers, thinkers, and speakers who act upon the supposition, of which Mill here gives us a glimpse, that property and vice go hand in hand; that the great object of the rich is, as it were, to injure their fellows, and that the richer they get and the more they spend the more they directly injure the poor. There has probably been no writer who deserves so much from society for exposing the absurdity of these sorts of ideas as

Charles Dickens, the moral of whose writings is that man's feelings and tendencies are the same in all grades of society. Riches are obtained by conformity to the scheme of society, he who conforms getting according to the amount of his conformity; and to abuse a man for compliance is foolish, and under the present scheme no one confers so much benefit on the poor as the rich, and no one confers so much benefit on the rich as the poor. The theory of consumption shows that the extinction of riches by saving must exterminate the poor. By inequality is the benefit conferred.

CHAPTER IV.

OF PROPERTY IN THE PRODUCTS OF LABOUR.

1. *Of the origin of property.*—The origin of the right to property may clearly be traced, as most people allow, to something very different from property itself, namely, the desire to repress crime. Mill, at Book II, chap. 1, sec. 2, of his "Principles of Political Economy," writes :—" Private property did not owe its origin to any of those considerations of utility which plead for the maintenance of it when established. Enough is known of rude ages, both from history and from analogous states of society in our own time, to show that tribunals (which always precede laws) were originally established not to determine rights, but to repress violence and terminate quarrels."

This shows us very clearly the reason of the institution of property, whether the property be real or personal, whether it be corporate or individual, corporeal or incorporeal. Man cannot progress at all until the right of his ownership to material objects be first not only admitted but enforced, and it is for the enforcement of this right among others that societies exist. Life progresses or retrogrades, as the interaction of the individuals subserves the interests of both or of one. It progresses most where the interests of both are subserved, but the interest of one more than that of the other.

No right to property is so readily conceded as that of the earnings of the individual to the results of his labour in commodities. The fact that man has endowed an object with a power of satisfaction, either of his own or his neighbour's wants, is sufficient to compel an assent to his right of property therein.

It is, however, the case that all matter on this earth is limited in amount, and consequently, to use the arguments of the communists, no one has any right to any material object more than another. We are placed by God in this earth, and this earth is the sum total of our inheritance; consequently no one has really any right to engross so much as the smallest grain of mustard seed without the consent either express or implied of his fellows.

Every right may be said to involve a wrong, or perhaps we should say that the wrong determines the right, and the fact that one man has engrossed any portion, however small, of the inheritance of all should make us study and try to understand why this wrong is permitted and what good is obtained by it. Search the world round and it will always be found that every proposition has a right and a wrong side, and however obvious the right, however consonant with reason and common sense, it is the business of any investigator not to write eulogies on the obvious, but to ask for reasons why the wrong is permitted, and whether the benefits obtained from that wrong more than counterbalance the injury.

Reasoners of the Bastiat type are much too fond of predicating, with an assumption of great knowledge, the blindness and ignorance of our ancestors of the bearing and effects of their actions. They assume for themselves the exclusive possession of knowledge. It is not going much too far to say that whatever was was right, that those things which people are apt to regard as the instances of the folly and stupidity of our ancestors, are really only proofs of the partial and incomplete knowledge of their descendants. In these days of scepticism we shall perhaps be laughed at for saying that every thing permitted by God to exist serves a purpose. What that purpose is, and how the result flows from the cause, is the business of man to find out.

Property in all things is a direct injury to our fellows, so the question to find out is why it is permitted, what purpose it serves, and how it serves that purpose, instead of blindly asserting a proposition, the truth of which no one would deny,—namely, the injury,—and then following it up with the *non sequitur*, therefore it must be abolished.

2. *Why it is permitted.*—Property is permitted for two reasons, it would seem: first, that man may increase and multiply, and secondly, that that increase may be attended with greater prosperity, or under improving conditions.

Supposing no property were permitted by man in anything, he would naturally follow out his animal instincts of preying upon his fellows. The great object of every man would be to take away what he saw any other man enjoying, that he might himself enjoy it; and such a pursuit of benefit as involves a disproportionate injury to some one else, must ultimately be attended with extinction of the race, or, at least, with its extreme restriction in numbers.

Again, property acts upon man as a stimulus to exertion. The savage who possesses nothing remains a savage because he posseses nothing, and it is in proportion to the fixation of property and its more clear recognition that civilization grows.

Perhaps no one has really illustrated the subject of property so well as Mr. Herbert Spencer, and a perusal of chap. 15 of his " Sociology " will illustrate better than anything the fact that a low state of civilization is the infallible accompaniment of a feeble sense of the right of property, and we quite agree with that learned writer when he says in section 576: "The fact referred in sec. 292 that even intelligent animals display a sense of proprietorship negatives the belief propounded by some that individual property was not recognized by primitive man."

It will no doubt by many be asserted that the cause of the clearer recognition of property was civilization, instead of the reverse being the case, but when we contemplate the history of any country it will generally be found that the following are the steps taken from anarchy or the practical application of the idea that might is right.

The oppression of the weak, the aged, and the young leads them to band together to secure the services of one more powerful than themselves in order to secure first their persons and then their property, and in proportion as they are able to enlist and to secure by payment the stronger party, they succeed in asserting their right, not only to their persons, but to their property, and so it ultimately becomes therefore the interest of the ruler to secure for them their rights than to reduce affairs to anarchy by plundering them.

There is probably no supposition so false and erroneous as that which asserts that the property of any given class has arisen from the plundering propensities of the men who formerly obtained it. As a matter of fact and history it will generally be found that what Herbert Spencer says in sec. 539

of his "Sociology," is the fact, that property arises from a state of militant activity, whether external or internal, but the facts have been, save in the case of the few lands confiscated on the conquest of any country, that the militant activity is internal, and second, that the militant party does not get the property.

The state of militant internal activity which must arise ultimately from communal property, is the cause of its being individualized. A certain amount of pressure, consequent upon the population increasing within a limited area, causes the militant activity which is ultimately repressed by the majority. The majority are seldom the plunderers, and it is only in times of total anarchy in the State that the plunderers, being in the majority, gain their object, so that to justify the statement of communists, that the original individual owners of property were plunderers of the public, it becomes necessary to prove a state of society when anarchy was raging fiercely and every man's hand was against his fellow. In any time of partial quiet and civilization plunderers do not really obtain property, save in very small and insignificant quantities. It is true that at the conquest of England a great many persons got property by forcible seizure with the king's consent or grant; but was not that a time of anarchy? And even then they got it as a return for services rendered to the bulk of the nation in enforcing peace under the feudal system, a system which, however oppressive it might be now, when the rights of property receive full recognition, was unquestionably well suited to the time.

The object attained by private property, whether it be real or personal, is the repression of the state of militant activity in most cases of internal militancy, that by its repression progress may be secured in populousness and wealth, and for this reason it is permitted.

Communistic arguments are merely specious disguises for producing anarchy so as to enable a certain class to obtain the possessions of their wiser and therefore wealthier neighbours.

3. *What purpose it serves.*—Private or individual property, whether it be real or personal, serves two objects—objects corresponding to the two persons which the right and the wrong involved in the idea clearly point out to us. It serves a purpose in relation to him that hath, and it serves a purpose in respect of him that hath not.

In regard to the former class, the words of the Bible may be aptly applied, "to him that hath shall be given," words which serve to indicate how property serves its purpose.

The ultimate object of all Political Economy should be to stimulate man's intellect, and property is one of the means made use of to effect that end.

Grant a man property in the results of his labour and he will probably be induced to increase his exertions, and he will, moreover, very soon discover that the more he exerts his mind in the matter the greater results will his labour attain. Property is the stimulus for saving ; it is, as Arthur Young said, the magic of property, which turns a barren waste into a garden. It is perhaps difficult to find out why property has this effect upon man in stimulating his exertions, unless it be that it enables him to regulate his idleness or enables him only to work when every thing favours his labour,—to watch every turn of the market with the power of stepping in at the right moment in order to get the most results. Whether we regard the market as nature's garden affected by the seasons, or the market for those stocks which are not natural productions, the idea by which property works is much the same.

Enough has been written upon this side of the question, too little upon the other save from the communistic point of view. The text above mentioned may be followed into this view, and it behoves man to ask why " from him that hath not shall be taken away."

The object served by property upon him that hath is obvious and simple, and it may be regarded first as teaching a lesson in morality and duty to those who have not. People who are without any property may trace their want of it to their own or their ancestors' indolence, ignorance, or folly. To indolence, in that they would not take the trouble to get; to ignorance, in that perhaps they were too idle to seek for the means of keeping; or to folly, in that they were too ready to spend the results of their own or some one else's labours.

There are, of course, cases of real hardship, or misfortune; but in many cases though hardship may be apparent at first sight, yet a closer inspection will lead us to a discovery of indolence either in mind or body as the real cause of poverty. The magic of property works upon those who have not, firstly, as a direct effect; and secondly, indirectly by enabling those who have to give labour a more remunerative direction. While not preventing the labour of those whose idleness, ignorance, or folly has rendered poor, it enables the rich to give their labour a more remunerative direction, so that while the labour of the poor and its results are not abstracted, the excess produced goes in remunerating the care and wisdom of the rich.

The capital of the rich which has been obtained by their labour and care is partly utilized by them in paying for fresh labour. Labour employs labour, and some capital employs labour, so that by granting to the careful man a property in the results of his labour, he is thereby enabled to employ further labour than before; so that that which was originally and directly as much injury to the poor as it was benefit to the rich has ultimately become a clear gain to the poor. The effect of property upon the rich directly and indirectly is obvious, and the effect indirectly upon the poor is obvious; not so obvious, however, is its directly beneficial effect. Property resembles to those who have it not the effect produced by a teacher upon his scholars who are without much desire to be taught; it stands before them (the poor) with a prize in one hand and a rod in the other. It says, in effect, your folly has rendered you poor, yet part of what you have refused to obtain shall be given back to you if you try to get it.

So far of the subjective purposes served by property. It is, however, necessary to consider the matter from the opposite point of view—namely, objectively, and it is this view which presents to us the greatest difficulty in considering the views of communists.

We have before adverted to the fact that man's effective demand is both absolutely limited and always satisfied; we have now to consider what effect the private property of some has upon those who are without any objects of property.

The remuneration given for the commodities which man effectively demands may be divided into two parts—namely, that part which goes to those who have property, that is to say, profit, and that which goes to labour, or those who have no property. The former class always come under the latter denomination so far as they obtain or consider themselves as obtaining a portion of the remuneration for their trouble in management; and this is commonly put down by business men at the present day at 5 per cent. upon their capital; till they have obtained more than that they will say they get no profit.

It is clear, then, that as the amount of the demand is fixed, the more capital put into any given business, the less amount must go to reward the labour unless there is a *pro tanto* reduction of profit. If, for instance, the amount given to remunerate the effective demand for bread in a week is £1,000,000, and the capital employed is the same amount and gets 20 per cent. or £200,000, then after deducting £5 per cent. for labour of superintendence, or £50,000, £850,000 goes in paying labour. Now, if the reward of capital should rise to 25 per cent., of course less goes to labour.

Supposing, however, that the effective demands of the producers do not rise, the extra profit becomes, in so far as it is capable of being employed reproductively, directly beneficial to those who have not property, for of any other employment to which that excess is applied some portion goes to remunerate fresh labour, and whether those who have not property or the labourers have benefited depends upon whether the amount of labour required reproductively exceeds the amount which has ceased to be required in the bread trade.

The extra profit can, however, be got in two ways, either by reducing the number of the labourers or the amount of their remuneration, the former of which may be injurious, while the latter must be.

From these considerations it will be seen that private property is to a certain extent working injury upon those who have not got it. Those who have it are perpetually striving to deduct some of the results of labour as profit, while the labour is always operating to force out the remuneration which property obtains. Two forces are striving for a larger portion of the total results produced, and the weaker and more ignorant goes to the wall because of that ignorance, and from inability to combine, consequent upon poverty. The outcome of the struggle is to raise the intellectual power and capacity of both parties; both get a reward, but the reward of the intellectually stronger is the greater of the two, and were the communists wise in their generation their object would be to cheat the rich, as it were, by either creating a fresh demand for commodities, or by causing a quicker transference of that demand from one commodity to another, by either of which means they would in effect be transferring more of the results of labour to the labouring classes, for every fresh demand would be a fresh outlet for labour, and every change of demand would produce more labour than it took away.

The injury to labour which property and the saving it causes, effects, depends upon two things: either upon the question, whether the increase in the effective demand and the consequent power of utilizing the savings is greater than the primary abstraction of labour by an application of such saving to the existing demand, or else upon the answer to the question, whether the saving of the poor is greater than that of the rich. If the labourers or those without property are able to save and so get part of the reward given for effective demand, then it stands to reason saving has not pecuniarily injured labour. We say pecuniarily, because if the labour of a country is lessening by so much, is its power and wealth being reduced? Less labour is not, as it is erroneously supposed to be, more wealth; but by how much greater the labour by which our wants are satisfied, by so much is the wealth of the country increased, for labour and wealth are nearly synonymous terms, as was seen when we were considering the word value.

4. *How it serves its purpose.*—Property, like wealth, is a mental idea materially expressed, and such being the case, it is, as it were, a confusion of opposites. Regard it subjectively, that is, from the view of mind, and it becomes clear that the more fixed and

certain it is materially, the better it expresses the idea.

Property viewed in this light may be said to be *par excellence* land and the three per cents. Nothing so well expresses to man's mind the idea property. The man who possesses these things in large quantities is always referred to as being a man of property. The power of the mind of the majority of human beings tends to fix the idea into the most fixed and certain objects.

Turn your view round however, and the return which property gives will show you just the opposite idea. What property gives a higher return than that which has a fluctuation in value? High interest is a sign of a bad or poor property. The mobility of the general mind in respect of the thing is the cause of this fluctuation in value. The question which we propose to answer is, then, which sort of property best serves its purpose as property.

So intense and powerful is the gambling spirit, which is merely a form of seeking the immaterial materially, that of the two views above referred to, the latter undoubtedly serves its subjective purpose best, and that is without doubt its chief purpose.

Nothing is so stimulating to man as a constant fluctuation in anything, and in the case of property, where there is great fluctuation, it renders the poor more able to become rich, and therefore brings riches within their reach. The object of property is to cause a perpetual struggle to obtain, at the same time giving good opportunities of obtaining, which fixity of property prevents. The sweet simplicity of the three per cents. is apt to cause an indolence which is fatal. The man whose wants are satisfied by merely going to receive his dividend, very soon ceases to trouble himself about increasing his property, and the struggle of individuals is the wealth-producer of the nation. The more therefore property becomes fixed, the more does it cease to serve its subjective purpose.

Objectively, however, the contrary is, of course, true. In property, man sees the means of holding in suspense his consumption, of rendering him able to consume in idleness the good things which his frugality has stored up, and the more fixed property becomes, therefore, the greater power of storage it possesses.

The man who has made a fortune after years of toil and labour, naturally seeks for that into which he can convert his property, with greater assurance of being able at any time to reconvert it, and to in any way take away from that power is to take away that which contributes, though only in the distance, to stimulate his exertions. If a man knew that the moment he was to cease labour all his property would vanish like chaff before the wind, there would be no stimulus to exertion, and he would be inclined to say to himself that exertion would be wasted upon accumulating that which he could not keep.

The result of these considerations then is to show that the great object to attain in respect of property is neither fixity nor fluctuation, but both—to get in equal quantities a fixed and a fluctuating form of property; and we see that man has attained to these forms of property, forms which the law has denominated real and personal, or objective and subjective property.

5. *Some considerations upon Communism, Socialism, &c.*—The above somewhat rudely sketched views in regard to property, coupled with our previous remarks upon exchange, enable us to deal with the questions as viewed by communists.

It will be seen that all questions of property have two sides to them, and that as you shut one eye and open the other, or reverse the operation, so will your view of the matter be. Keep away from your view the subjective object at which property aims, and you must be logically a communist, for if property has no object or result in moving man, then property is a most unmitigated evil.

Reverse the operation and you will see that the *summum bonum* which the idea property was to attain, was best attained under a feudal system, a system which caused the greatest fixity of property.

It is needless to say that both views are true, but are not the whole truth, and are very far from being nothing but the truth, because they are one-sided. In olden time the feudal system was necessary, useful, and beneficial in repressing internal as well as external militancy. In more modern times its relaxation was beneficial, because the object—namely, fixity—could be attained without it.

The object of communism is to abstract what we may call the grinding power from property,—that power which enables the possessor of it, whether it be lands or shares, to draw to themselves the unearned increment, that is to say, the increment which arises from an increasing population. It may be useful here, just to point out, in the first place, that communists carefully shut their eyes to the fact that such unearned increment is always divided between those who have and those who have not property, though we may admit that those who have property get the lion's share. Considering what we have said before, it follows naturally that this, which is regarded by shutting one eye as an unmitigated evil, is, when we open the other, just the very object which property was instituted to obtain.

Property was instituted in order that its owners might, by getting the unearned increment, be induced to strive for more, and we may say with the knowledge that this very unearned increment which seems so unjust would end ultimately in benefiting those from whom it was apparently at first taken away, but who in reality would never have got it had no property been permitted in it.

If, for instance, the unearned increment, say in the rent of land, was transferred to the State, the rate of interest expected on an investment in land would rise at once, for people would cease to invest in that which involved great trouble and bother in looking after, and only yielded, notwithstanding, a fixed and certain rate of profit.

It may be plausibly argued that people would still save and economize notwithstanding the abstraction of the unearned increment, but the abstraction of the stimulus is tantamount to the abstraction of the thing itself. If there were no profits in gambling no one would gamble, and were there no unearned increments half, and from the mercantile point of view all, the profits would be gone.

It cannot, we think, be denied, that the possessors of property get more of the unearned increment than those who have none, and that is the supposed injury at which communism aims. Now suppose, for a moment, that the excess was transferred to the State by any of the schemes which have been devised, it is not going too far to say that there would then be no excess or unearned increment at all. Transferring it to the State is merely a device for its abolition—we mean a device for getting rid of the increment, and not as is supposed for causing it to be earned.

That which the State had power to take from the community, the community would very soon wrest from the State. Suppose a law passed that all rent above the rent of a fixed day was to be paid to the State, by what possible machinery would rent be raised? No one save a small minority of State officers could raise it, and popular clamour would soon put them down. Every individual would see half a hundred very clear reasons why to suppose any unearned increment was impossible and ridiculous.

But it will be said there must be an increment even though the Government could not get it. This is entirely false. The unearned increment would be dissolved in idleness, less exertion would be needed, and less wealth would result. Every householder, *i.e.*, the majority of the population, would relax his efforts just in proportion to the amount of the unearned increment, or, in this case, the non-existing increment; the increment would be turned into a decrement.

The State uses property as a machine to enable one class to grind the other so that both may benefit, and were the grinding power transferred to the State it would cease to exist. Communism is veiled anarchy.

In Book II, chapter i, sec. 3, of his "Principles of Political Economy," J. S. Mill writes:—"The objection ordinarily made to a system of community of property and equal distribution, that each person would be incessantly occupied in evading his fair share of work, points undoubtedly to a real difficulty;" and then he goes on to say that they who urge this objection forget that the same difficulty exists under the present system. With all due respect to Mr. Mill, no sensible person forgets it at all; instead of forgetting it they would point to the fact that by means of a small inequality originally permitted—that is to say, by allowing a profit on labour—half the community is engaged in watching and squeezing as much work as they can from the other half, a duty which cannot be so well performed by State officials who have no direct interest in performing it. Moreover, the squeezing of one portion of the community by the other does ultimately benefit the other, for they are rewarded according to the labour which they give, and if moved sufficiently by self-interest they have the power to transpose themselves from the one class to the other. The evil of communism is, that it endeavours to abolish self-interest; and to suppose man can in his present state of life get rid of all desire whatever to benefit himself seems to us radically absurd, and that no good would result assuming it to be accomplished.

It is true under the present system the position of matters economical is reversed, and that whereas uncivilized man worked for others—that is, his descendants through himself; whereas civilized man works for himself through others—that is, his neighbours; but whether civilized or uncivilized man works ultimately for self, self is the motor power whether it be expressed in one form or another, and to suppose an abstraction of self is to suppose creation on a fresh plan.

6. *Of the reasons for permitting private property in land.*—It need hardly be said that the reasons for permitting private property in land have been very inefficiently enumerated by economists. Mill says that the reason for permitting it is in order that those who improve it may reap the benefit of their improvements, see Book II, chapter ii, sec. 5. To draw any conclusions from such a view of the case seems almost like a desire to beg the question, for it can hardly be regarded as essential to the power of reaping the results of improvements that there should be private property in land. Mr. Gladstone's Irish Land Bills have shown that such a conclusion from such premisses is not permissible.

In the first place, then, we may premise that, deductively considered, there is no more reason why private property should be denied in the case of land any more than in anything else. I, individually, have a right to exist, and that right is only available for me as long as I can obtain the means of subsistence; however great my powers of labour may be without land it is impossible that I can exist, and therefore, unless you deny my right to existence, you cannot logically take away from me the right of possession of the means of existence.

But, considered inductively, inasmuch as there are hundreds of others besides myself who have a like right whom the admission of mine must exclude, it seems perhaps only reasonable that my right should be disallowed, or allowed only communally—that is, with the others.

By regarding these two considerations together, as is necessary to a complete view, and considering also the fact that there are inequalities in soils, whether in regard to produce or position, it will be seen that the first object to secure in the case of land is the repression of militancy, as before alluded to. The first question which here arises is as to the manner how.

In the case of small societies occupying a large area the inducements to dispute the possession of any particular portion are small in proportion as the excess of land in its productive capacity exceeds the total numbers of its settlers. At such times, as Sir Henry Maine and others have shown, landed property was held by the commune, and pieces were granted out to each individual of the clan who possessed it. Every man had his right to live and no one suffered wrong.

This primitive condition of man was undoubtedly dissolved by the community for its own good, and from its dissolution sprang private property in land. The justification of the right of private property is public convenience, and it has no ground of justification in the right to improvements conferred by the individual on the soil. Public peace and profit are the justification of landed property. A growing and large community upon a small area compel the right to private property to be recognized, in order that disputes as to possession may be settled; and, secondly, the greater exertion which man is willing to lay out on his own leads to a greater profit being obtained from it.

Mill, in accordance with his system, carefully reverses the true reason for private property in land as in other things. The justification lies not in the effects produced by man upon land in consequence of private property, but the effects produced by private property in land upon man. The reason is subjective, not objective. The first justification is the production by it of peace among men, the second is the production of more labour among men, and so more benefit to his fellow man.

Another and equally important reason for permitting private property in land is, that by so doing man is enabled to invest his labours in it with the confident expectation that they will not be abstracted in consequence of his ceasing to labour. It supplies a form of investment to a purchaser which would be withdrawn were landed property held by the public. It is one of the great public accumulators, and as such has a great effect in stimulating consumption.

The man whose savings are invested in a good permanent security is far more ready to benefit his fellows by increasing his consumption, and his ability and power of doing so is rendered greater in proportion to the fixity of the term of his investment. To the objective economists such an object of course is ridiculous and absurd, its validity depends upon the system or object of Political Economy.

The fact that private property in land works hardship and injustice is no doubt to a small extent true, and that is just the reason why it should be kept up, for the hardship and injustice must come in any case, and under the present system such hardship is reduced to a minimum, while the community gets the greatest possible amount of benefit.

7. *Of the cause of rent.*—In the preceding section we have alluded, to a certain extent, to the origin of rent. Rent, in its inception, was undoubtedly the recognition of communal possession of the right of property in the soil consequent upon its ceasing to be practically communal property while it remained so in theory.

There is no doubt, or very little now, as Sir Henry Maine and others have shown, that among the Aryan tribes landed property was originally both possessed and divided communally, and in order that that division might be carried out each community, upon settling on a piece of land, put a limit upon the quantity which they fixed on their inheritance, and then divided it up among all the members at different periods, so that each man's possession only lasted for a certain time. It is needless to remark that such an arrangement could only serve during very primitive times; to divide, for instance, the land of this country equally among its inhabitants would be a labour impossible, because of its magnitude.

Seeing that this perpetual redivision could not last long, both on account of its tendency to produce strife for certain portions and to paralyze the labours of the community for a considerable period,—for in proportion as the time for redivision arrived man's labours would relax, the abstraction of a portion of their result being imminent,—it became necessary to provide a means of individualizing property. It was not, however, therefore necessary that the idea of communal property should be given up, and the struggle to confer private property in land and at the same moment to deny it, resulted in the bringing forth of rent, or the acknowledgment of the communal right.

That this was the origin of rent the feudal system

and the laws of this country tend to show. The law of England declares that freeholders are merely free tenants, tenants or holders of land from the sovereign, and originally there seems but little doubt that every freeholder paid rent to the sovereign, or what would in those days of payment in kind be regarded as rent. The greater lords under the feudal system all acknowledged their tenure from their sovereign, they paid rent, suit, or service as it was lawfully demanded.

No man in the country was permitted absolute power over his land, all were ultimately in subjection to the sovereign, and the sovereign to the people.

The services or rents of the greater lords tended to extinction in consequence of their irksomeness, increasing in proportion to their smallness and want of value to the recipient, or from their being bought of the crown in its necessities; but for all that they must be regarded both as practically existent in the rent of to-day, and as evidence of the right of the individual to the land being subject merely to the convenience and benefit of the State, of that benefit and how it is conferred, enough has been said.

So far for the subjective view or rent as arising from the interaction of men. We now come to the objective view or rent from the consideration of the interaction of commodities, or things in exchange.

8. *Of the cause of the rise in rent.*—The rise of rent

is due to the different values of objects or commodities when exchanged. The greater the value in exchange of the commodities which the soil produces, or may be considered to produce, the greater the rise of rent. By considered to produce, it is meant, or intended to be understood, that all labour which produces an exchangeable commodity—be it law, commerce, or mining—raises the rent.

We have previously pointed out that value, like wealth, is originally a subjective idea, which becomes objective simply by the introduction of exchange. There are two things which raise value, limit in quantity and immateriality, and these two things are the motor powers in any rise of rent.

The secondary object of rent is to produce equality. Equality by re-division being disposed of, it became necessary to obtain equality somehow, and it was got by altering and adjusting the rent paid by landholders in proportion to the results, which they obtained from the use of the properties in the soil. It naturally followed that the more fertile land was, the higher rent it had to pay. Fertility, however, depends not upon the cultivator, but upon the wants of the people for whom the land is cultivated. However naturally fertile land may be, it can command no rent save subjective or nominal rent, unless the produce is capable of being consumed by someone.

A consideration of the two motor powers in value

above mentioned will show that in regard to rent, the more material the produce of the land becomes, the greater is the power of raising rent given by limit in quantity; whereas the more immaterial the produce, the less power has limit of quantity in causing a rise of rent or altering the value.

Take, for instance, the produce of agriculture, and suppose an average production and consumption, and consequently a medium rent, then rent rises in proportion to the limitation of the quantity of produce; such limitation may, however, take place, in consequence not simply of less being produced, but either by more being wanted for consumption, or the difficulties of consumption being increased, as by distance, want of efficient means of transport, etc.

Take the case of coal mining, and the result will be much the same; the moment there is a limit in quantity, up goes the rent, though of course where rent is fixed and arranged at stated intervals it does not feel the effects of the limit so quickly.

In gold mining, however, rent if it was paid would remain tolerably well fixed, as is shown by the stability in the value of gold, notwithstanding the periodically enormous discoveries such as those of Australia and California. The power of limit in quantity in raising rent varies inversely as the immateriality of the product.

The reason of this rise of rent is, as we pointed

out before, that there is a greater excess of supply being produced; consequent upon the exchange more commodities are being given to purchase the product in question, and that extra quantity the landlords deduct for the benefit of the community.

It is not to be supposed that they withhold it from the community, for such an idea would be absurd in the highest degree; it is either productively or reproductively consumed; but the excess being passed from the immediate producers to the landlords, prevents those immediate producers from relaxing their efforts to produce a further supply for the community, and causes them still to labour by filtering the produce through other channels.

Immateriality in the product of labour is the source of the continued rise of rent, as is shown in large cities where rent rises in business quarters. The functions of merchants, traders, lawyers, and bankers, is not with the material objects which are consumed or intended for consumption, so much as with the facilitating and transfer of those material objects. To say such functions are immaterial would sound like a statement of their inutility, which is not intended at all. It will, we think, be conceded that the less business men have to do with the objects of commerce—that is, the farther off from their transactions the objects are removed—the greater are the profits they get.

A vast amount of profit is made by bankers; brokers, stockbrokers, and others who only deal with the papers which afford a title to the object dealt in many of them, probably hardly see the goods they are dealing with, and it seems not going too far to say that the more immaterial the service, the greater is the profit and the consequent rise in rent.

But perhaps we are going too far into the regions of speculation to please the majority of readers.

It is sufficiently obvious that it is more difficult to duly estimate rent in the case of cities, and where rent rises, as we have said, from the immateriality of the produce than in the case of agriculture or mining, for so much depends upon the power of brain. Two men who occupy similar premises in a city alongside of one another, will make a very different profit in the course of one year, and it is consequently only possible to estimate the rent they should pay very roughly. Moreover, were they made strictly to pay according to profit, the one who paid most would probably quit possession as soon as possible, and take his business where his labours could get more reward.

Again, another instance of the power of immateriality in raising rent is afforded in the case of the rents of houses in the fashionable quarters of any town. Why does rent rise so in these places, towards which fashion turns the tide of population?

In any case the reasons are generally immaterial. The view, the neighbourhood, and the neighbours, and a hundred other reasons are given which it would be absurd to class as utilities fixed and embodied in material objects. The pleasures of sense in one form or another is the sole reason.

9. *Of peasant proprietors.*—In respect of peasant proprietors, it need hardly be said, two points of view must be considered, namely :—the subjective and objective before any just decision can be come to upon the point.

It is useless to show—that is from the humanitarian point of view simply—that more is obtained from the cultivating the soil under peasant proprietorship than under the system of large holdings.

Having proved, or being supposed to have proved, that peasant proprietors get more from the soil than larger holders, it yet remains to be shown that the conditions of life are rendered in any way easier, happier, and more productive of large minded views and toleration.

It is very questionable whether actually more is produced under peasant proprietorship, and after reading Mill's remarks on the subject at Book II, chap. vi, one is only tempted to favour it in out of the way corners of any country—in districts which, in consequence of their inaccessibility to commerce, are rendered vacant under the system of large holdings by the smallness of their return and the distance from a market. Large holdings in these sort of spots are rendered useless by the abstraction of consumers, which a peasant proprietorship would introduce. More persons would be required to cultivate them, and more consumers would result. The great evil, if such one may term it, of large holdings is, that the produce is vastly in excess of the number of consumers, and unless some city is nigh at hand to receive the excess and give a return for it, the producing power is wasted.

The great evil of peasant proprietors which objective economists fail to notice, is that it tends to produce retrogression in thought and action among the proprietors. There is no exchange, in consequence of the near approach of effective demand to production, and the surplus is so small which each individual can obtain from his exertions, that capital augments but slowly.

Again, exchange of goods involves exchange of thought and unity of action; it promotes good by bringing men together and making the interest of each subservient to the interest of the whole number. Where each man is fixed upon his own plot of land and never moves off, his ideas at once begin to assume a somewhat similar limit, and he has no thought save whether he will be able to produce enough for the morrow.

It follows also that towns would, under this

system, die out from lack of sustenance, and retrogression would commence in the cities as well as the country. It is only by the vast increase in the producing over the consuming powers of the country, as distinguished from the towns, that permits of the existence of the towns at all, for towns cannot produce their own sustenance. By differentiation or inequality, by town and country does the wealth increase, so that in the neighbourhood of large towns large holdings seem to be not only natural but useful.

The Western States of America, for instance, are held and cultivated on a large scale, chiefly in consequence of the density and town-like consistency of England. Enormous quantities of wheat and agricultural produce generally are produced in excess of the consumption of those states, and were it not for that excess London would hardly be able to increase at all.

To go fully into the matter would involve statistics which are not to hand, and we have merely appended these remarks on the subject because they seem rendered necessary in consequence of the smallness of the views taken up by either party, as they advocate large or small holdings.

10. *Of property in the improvements in material agents.*—This is perhaps the latest subject of property which civilization produces. Property in

the products of mind as expressed in matter, and it takes various forms. Patent laws are the guarantee of property in some of these products, but improvements in land, which must come under the same head, have not the same guarantee, and this because of the greater compulsion which one party to the matter exerts upon the other in their adoption and use. An inventor of any kind does not in any way compel the public to use his invention. He is, as it were, the suitor to the public. He asks them to recompense him for the benefit which he has conferred, or thinks he has conferred, upon the public. If, however, a tenant-farmer wishes to improve his material agents of production, then he is, by the very nature of his improvement, not only compelled to use some one else's property to do it, but he uses force to obtain its introduction. He, to a certain extent, is compelled to violate an existing right, which an ordinary machine inventor need not do, though if he does litigation generally results.

Considering what has been said as to the rights of property in land as to the ultimate undoubted and acknowledged right of the community to land, it seems to suggest itself to one that a set of land commissioners might very well be established who would regulate and provide for tenants' rights in improvements in land, commissioners whose business it would be first to ascertain whether tenants should be allowed to improve the property of their landlords—that is, of course, in the event of any objection on the landlord's part,—and, secondly, to determine also, in the event of dispute, how much and in what form the tenant's improvement should be returned to him.

The principle of compelling people to reduce rents is a principle which strikes at the root of all private property, and is more injurious to the public at large than to the landlords; though at first sight the injury may not seem very obvious, it is injurious to the public, for it is simply allowing, nay, assisting, the idleness and incompetence of tenants to assert itself more fully, and so conducing to public starvation. The object in view in any legislation should be the more clear assertion of private rights, the foundation of society; and the suggestion contained above is merely made with that object in view. High rent is a public benefit, and the object of legislation should be to keep up and keep intact every individual right so long as the benefit is greater than the injury caused by so doing. The legislation proposed above would have for its object the greater benefit of tenants than injury to landlords. Every interference with landlords' property is an injury not merely to the landlords, but the public. The public have, however, a claim upon that property, and if legislation can be proposed which will benefit them more than it benefits landlords, then such legislation is desirable.

We can conceive no reason why, as a matter of justice, a tenant should not have a right of property in his improvements, and no reasonable man would refuse it; but it does not therefore follow that one man should be able to compulsorily improve another man's property and then sell to that other man, or some one else, those improvements. Moreover, it seems only reasonable that as patent law protects improvements in some material agents it should also protect improvements in others.

The great difficulty in the matter consists in the fact that the improvements are fixed in the agents and cannot be parted from them in being dealt with, but a land company might very well be started with sufficient capital which would buy all tenants' improvements other than those which the landlord would be disposed or able to purchase, and would be empowered to charge a rent for those improvements, to be paid by the tenant for similar terms of years and restrictions to those granted under the present patent law to inventors.

Improvements in land and improvements in machinery do not differ from one another when regarded objectively, or as respects increased production. All the difference seems to us to lie solely in the compulsion put upon others in their adoption, and that is a matter which the community have an interest in discussing.

Political Economy deals solely with the benefit or injury derived from improvements in material agents, so that a disquisition upon the law would be out of place. The economic aspects of the question are continually under discussion, their importance being generally admitted.

The question from an economical point of view is whether or not the country benefits by allowing a property in them, and it seems almost universally conceded that it does.

CHAPTER V.

OF CAPITAL.

1. *What is capital?*—Like almost every economical question, hardly two people will agree as to what they mean by capital, and one has only to read Mill carefully to see that his ideas, although fully expressed in the chapters which deal with it, were none the less fluctuating when he confines himself to the use of the word. Sometimes he means a store, sometimes he means money, and sometimes he means things employed in production; he has no more settled idea, we might also say less settled idea, than an ignorant man from the street who knows nothing of economy.

Now in order to settle the question, there seem but two methods to be employed—either, first, to explain how capital arises or what causes it; and, secondly, without considering that matter, to see what implications language in common use gives.

Professor Hearn kindly answers our first question straight off, on page 136 of his "Plutology," he says:—"How then did capital begin? If its presence be essential to industry, how could industry have originated? To such questions there are no means of reply. The earliest records of our race imply the existence of capital."

This answer from such an authority seems to us conclusive. Economists tell you what capital is; they cannot tell us how we come by it.

Now turn to the other point—namely, the use of the vulgar tongue by the people, and see what that tells you.

A B goes to discuss with a friend his son's entry into a business, and he says:—" I am quite willing to put some capital into a good business if I can only find one. I would put in £2000 or £3000." Can you imply from this that capital means anything else than money, or are we misusing our native tongue in so constructing the sentence? Does A B mean from those words that he will put in, as Professor Price says, "wealth employed in producing fresh wealth?" It seems to us that he could not put in what was already in that business or some other. How is a man to transfer a weaving machine into a brewery, and if he did what good would come of it?

Or take another case: A banker asserts at a dinner-table that there is at the present time a vast quantity of unemployed capital, and he is taken to task by an economist for misusing words, who, to show him his error, says, What do you mean by unemployed capital? Whereupon the banker replies, I mean that bankers have more to lend than they can find borrowers for. Surely the only inference possible is, that the banker, when he says capital, means money, and not steam engines, spades, and food.

Other cases might be multiplied *ad libitum*. The use of the English language is such that we may rely upon it as furnishing incontestible evidence that the man who speaks of capital means, save among savages, money and nothing else.

We invest our capital in "shoes or ships or sealing-wax," and what it is invested in is not the thing, any more than our bodies are clothes because they are invested in them. If I invest my capital in a brewery, the brewery is that which represents it by vats and other machinery and tools.

Exchange with money involves a double transmutation from commodity to money and from money to the things employed reproductively, and, as curious instances of the perversity of the human mind, ideas upon capital are unsurpassed.

Economists like to return to savagery and to abolish the interim transmutation; they persist in tacking the word capital on to the ultimate object of transmutation; but there are other thinkers, such as Mr. Ruskin, who, equally objecting to call the middle object of transmutation capital, are desirous to attach it to the untransmuted commodity, who, like Mill sometimes, call capital the store, but deny to it the form which their language compels them to put upon it. Every man who thinks upon the subject is primarily unanimous in discarding the idea money, and so they are all at variance as to whether transmutation has anything to do with the idea.

A friend, with whom we discussed the matter, said that he thought capital was merely our way of regarding commodities. Like Mr. Ruskin, he thought capital was simply an untransmuted store of goods or commodities, and that he who possessed a saleable article possessed capital to the extent of its saleability.

All this confusion arises from the objective method of regarding exchange. In asserting that exchange is the result of equality the whole question has been thrown into the direst confusion. Look at exchange subjectively and you cannot, unless you are blind, fail to perceive inequality, and that inequality, the producer of profit, is also the producer of capital. By inequality we cause it to grow.

2. *Of the production of capital.*—As is obvious, we differ from Professor Hearn and all other economists in asserting, first, that money is capital; and second, that its production can be traced accurately even in those cases where, there being no money, capital is not money.

Capital is produced under either of two conditions: it is produced either under exchange, as in all civilized communities at the present day—that is, altruistically; or it may be produced egoistically—

that is, among savages, where no exchange or barter exists at all.

Let us begin with the latter, production, and suppose a man to betake himself to the wilds of a country one hundred miles from his fellows; how does he, under those circumstances, get capital?

The first thing to consider is, how much he wants for productive consumption. In the case of most crops, like wheat, only one crop a year is produced, and so the man has to consider how he is to exist until he obtains a crop at all; he cannot live for a year upon nothing or in a desert, so that it must be supposed he chooses a spot where there is a banyan tree or some fruit producer. The first thing he will do will be to pluck all the ripe fruit and store it for his winter consumption; he will collect all he can till he thinks he has got enough to live upon until next year, and that is his capital. He sets to work to obtain a supply in excess of his present need for productive consumption, and that excess is his capital. All through the winter, and until the recurring season have brought a fresh crop, he has his wants satisfied; and if he be not a drone of the hive during that period when he might be idle if he chose, he can labour at the production of something other than that which will immediately produce a satisfaction; but if he does so he will not call that something which he then produces his capital, but the store which he has gathered. Egoistically, then, capital is an excess of supply beyond productive consumption.

There is, however, another point to consider; a man in this condition cannot precisely tell how much he will want to consume in the given period for which he collects this store, and if he is a wise man he will get more than he thinks he can possibly need during that period. The same principle is carried out in victualling any ship—the supply is made to exceed the probable demand; and although during the first period of savagery the name capital may be applied to the whole store in excess of the demand of the moment, yet as time gets on it is limited to the amount which the man, if he is careful, has over at the end of the year, which must necessarily elapse before a second supply of commodities is produced.

During the whole of the period of consumption without production—that is, the winter—the man may have produced a bow and arrows or a canoe, or a hundred other things, but he would not call them his capital unless he could sell them.

If he produced them with that object, then it is possible to consider them capital; by doing so, however, he does not render unnecessary to the idea, capital, excess of supply, but merely gives the name to the result instead of the cause, so that capital when produced in savagery is excess of supply, but when produced by exchange it should be described as the result of such excess.

Under exchange, or in cases of the altruistic production of capital, it is more properly called the result of excess of supply. Having in the case supposed collected enough for a year's consumption, the man by creating a fresh product, which he is able to exchange, by that exchange adds to his capital. His capital becomes not only excess of supply, but the result of labour at production in excess of that excess. His capital is augmented by his working when he might be idle.

It remains to consider what effect money would have on the production of capital.

Supposing this man to have been an ordinary farmer, instead of hoarding up his grain as capital in a barn he would take it at once to market and sell it, and instead of its being said then, as Mr. Ruskin would have it, that his store of grain was his capital, he would call his money which he got for it his capital. The fact that his capital was grain and is money does not the less make it capital, and instead of his capital being that which would satisfy his definite wants for a definite time, it is now able to satisfy his indefinite wants for an indefinite time.

But there are a class of persons who are not content with the English language, and one transmutation but must needs have two, and make the second one take a definite form; a totally unnecessary proceeding as far as we can see, and would compel our farmer to spend his money before he would be entitled to call it his capital.

Capital then is excess of supply beyond the amount necessary for the productive consumption of any given period, be it a week, a month, a year, or a day.

Under the ordinary exchange of common life it arises in consequence of the inequality. The producer of goods or the seller of them, by getting more than he gave, gets an excess of supply, and he may either spend that excess or not as he chooses; but if he does spend it, it becomes evident he will not become a capitalist. Transmutation, which was unnecessary to the idea when life was carried on in a primitive manner, becomes essential as progress is secured, and money becomes the measure and transmitter of goods.

We have, however, remarked that whereas capital under primitive ideas was only capable of satisfying man's indefinite wants, by exchange into money it becomes capable of satisfying man's indefinite wants. The man whose capital was a store of corn could only make use of that corn in a certain limited manner, whereas when he has got money for it there is no limit to the sorts of things which he can buy with it, and this alteration in power of purchase and applicability we render by the word condense. So that the proper definition of capital, like the proper definition of a seed, is that result of excess of supply which by transmutation is condensed.

The power or applicability is that which the word capital seeks to denominate. Capital is that which a man can apply in any manner he chooses, and therefore it must be excess of supply for the supply necessary for his productive consumption he cannot utilize, unless he wishes to starve. The difference between our idea of capital and Mill's for instance, is that whereas Mill says capital is that which is applied, we say capital is that which has the most universal power of being applied.

It is a great pity that economists should ignore the power of money, for there is nothing which is so obvious to the meanest person, and to suppose the majority are not the best judges of what money is and does, seems like getting ready for a fall. Professor Price, for instance, regards money as a cart or truck, a mere means of conveying goods from A to B, but that is a very narrow and contracted view of the subject. Money can be turned into everything, but everything certainly cannot be turned into money.

According to the orthodox economist, capital ceases to be capital the moment it is unemployed, for the definitions given are things employed in production. So that if I have a weaving shed, and a lock-out take place, I lose my capital, an assertion most persons would deny.

But as we have pointed out before, the definitions of economists will not bear either critical inspection or common use. They arise from trying to simplify the complex, when the complexity is the idea wanted.

3. *Of the limit to the creation of capital.*—At first sight it would seem that there is no limit to the amount of the capital that may be created, but a few moments' consideration will show that the amount created must be limited, and it will further lead to the conclusion that although at times it may be created in excess of its capability of employment, yet such excess cannot last very long, and it will be absorbed either in reduction of the rate of interest, that is, in stopping the further production of capital, or in productive or reproductive consumption.

The latter forms of employment are the best, for reduction of interest is a reduction of the stimulus to trade.

The profits in all businesses tend to reduction in consequence of the competition, and that tendency limits the production of capital; but a countervailing influence is always at work, more particularly in this country of speculative companies, to absorb the excess of capital in new fields of enterprise. It is a great benefit to England its possessing so many and such prosperous colonies, for they are ever ready to absorb increasing supplies of capital, and the return to this country of successful colonists is not so very detrimental to the colonies themselves as may at first sight be supposed, for these returned colonists, finding the home rate of interest too low to please them, afford assistance from their knowledge to those who are anxious to start new enterprises abroad, and the injury really results in benefiting the colonies themselves.

The amount of capital may be said to be limited by the effective demand for productive and reproductive consumption, though it is the case that it very often exceeds both, but when it does so the state of plethora brings its own cure in the stagnation of trade resulting therefrom, production is carried on either at a loss or at the very smallest perceptible profit, just so much as will keep production going until the excess is absorbed. It is, however, at this excess that many of the bubble companies may be said to be aimed, and aimed in many cases most successfully.

This plethora of capital is very injurious to the working classes, for it becomes the object of producers to get rid of as many hands as they possibly can, so as to get more profit from cheaper production, and no state of society can be better studied as a refutation of the eternity argument of Mr. J. S. Mill concerning capital employing labour, than these periodic fits of plethora of capital, for they should, if Mill's arguments were true, go simply to benefit the labourer which they most certainly do not.

Take, for instance, the recent period, or 7 or 10, through which this country has been passing when there has been an acknowledged plethora of capital, and no sane person would attempt to assert that that supply of capital has been the unmitigated boon which Mill would make it out to be. The demand for productive and reproductive consumption fell far short of the supply of commodities and capital, and the result has been that manufacturers have been glad if they could only just hold their heads above water, and not be compelled to close their mills altogether, in the same way that farmers have been compelled to give up farming; and we cannot but think that had farming been rendered a capital producing occupation by protection, a great portion of the idle capital would have been first absorbed in making it pay, and both the manufacturers and farmers would have benefited. The capital absorbed by farming would have raised up a supply of customers for the manufacturers, and the original injury which would be worked by the primary imposition of a small tax on food, would in an incredibly short space of time have resulted in a vast benefit to the nation.

If economists will persist with the eternity argument, that is to say, that there being an unlimited demand for manufactures, you could buy with them just as powerfully under Free Trade as protection it is useless to discuss the question, but inasmuch as we consider the demand for manufactures to be limited, a plethora soon results, and their purchasing power is gone, so that while you are, as in the case of England, unable to produce bread, you are at the same time precluded from buying with cotton shirtings, and the end is stagnation and starvation.

The question to put to this country is, simply the question whether economy is to be subjective or objective, that is to say, do we buy with cotton shirtings because some one else wants to have them, or do we buy with them because we have chosen to produce them; the question is simple and obvious, and is an every day question answered readily by any man of business, and with the public we leave it. Is a mess of pottage as good and useful as a birth-right?

4. *Is capital saved?*—Nothing is more astonishing and affords a clearer proof of the eternity arguments of objectivists than their statement that capital is the result of saving. They suppose that man's effective demand for productive consumption is unlimited, and then say that by limiting that effective demand, he will be able to save some portion of the things he produces and turn them into capital, or to consume them reproductively. It seems to us that they entirely beg the question, and that so far from capital being the result of saving, it is more truly denominated, particularly when produced by

exchange, the result of spending, and that saving is only applicable to its egoistic production.

To save means not to consume, and how not consuming is to produce capital we are utterly at a loss to conceive. Capital is the result of producing more than you want to consume in a given time, and only by perverting the meaning of the word save, and saying that it means consuming less than you produce, can capital be said to be saved.

However much the word save may be applicable to the production and consumption of one man, it certainly is no proper description of capital as produced under exchange. Saving can by no stretching of the word mean the spending by A of more than B consumes, which is the cause of the production of capital by exchange. Another difficulty which arises in considering the matter is, that according to Mill, an excess of supply is an irrational and absurd doctrine, and yet capital is saved; one would have thought that saving cannot take place without the existence of an excess to save; nothing is so irrational as what must occur is the only permissible conclusion. But Mill gets us out of the dilemma by saying "there are other cases in which the term saving, with the associations usually belonging to it, does not exactly fit, the operation by which capital is increased;" and further on, "nevertheless there is an increase of saving in the scientific sense."

We think, then, that to use the word save in a

treatise on economy in a scientific sense is to misuse the word. To use the vulgar tongue with a concealed meaning is to impose on the reader; and to say there is nothing to save and yet there is saving sounds very like nonsense, and consequently there never was a more untrue statement than that of Mill's, that spending impoverishes the nation as well as the individual. Spending is the source both of wealth and capital.

With Mill's famous argument concerning excess of supply, and his interesting division of purchase power into desire to possess and means of purchase, we have, perhaps, already said enough; but we think it cannot be too fully impressed on the reader that so far as subjective economy is concerned some one else's desire to possess is my means of purchase, and that to divide the power of purchase is impossible in reality, however much theorizers may succeed in splitting it. Some one else's desire for my sovereign, or the things he can get for it, is that which makes my sovereign buy; and that possession of a house, for instance, which no one will purchase, cannot fairly be said to be the possession of a commodity; to call it a commodity is to trifle with words. So that from the subjective view Mill's argument is absurd.

5. *Of the altered circumstances of the production of capital.*—The production of capital in these days of

rapid communication has to some extent altered from the more primitive production of it, and whereas among our ancestors inequality between the amount produced and the amount paid by consumers was alone relied on as the producing cause of capital, now producers have to rely not merely on this inequality, but in the more rapid production of it.

That is to say, that whereas in the slow times of 200 years ago, a man turned over his capital once or twice in a year, now reliance is placed more upon the rapidity of turn over; and men like Stuart, the New York millionaire, are content with 10 per cent. if they can only get it quick enough, say six times in a year.

Another circumstance also which requires to be noticed is, that the quantity of goods bought and sold to get a profit becomes much more vast, and enormous sums of capital have to be invested if any profit is to be made by its use. It is to this extension of the amount of capital utilized that the modern joint stock companies are owing. The capital embarked becomes so great that men do not like to venture single-handed into a concern which may bring ruin on their families from very slight causes, and they are not so ready to embark the great masses of capital alone and with unlimited responsibility.

The tendency of the former alteration in the

production of capital is undoubtedly unfavourable to the working population, more strain is put upon them in production, and the capitalists find it more difficult still to make a profit, and consequently are always looking out for opportunities of getting rid of as many hands as they can possibly do without. There is, however, no evil which is not mitigated in some way, and cheaper goods to a certain extent benefit the poor, though naturally not so much as they do the rich, for they are less able to take advantage of the cheapness.

This increasing rapidity in the turn over of the capital invested in trade has been productive of middle men, who form, as it were, a sort of channel through which the goods pass on their way from the producer to the consumer. Warehousemen spring up, who buy from producers wholesale and more readily than the public, and so enable the manufacturer to keep going perhaps during the fall of the ultimate market.

It is not to be supposed that the warehousemen lose by their transactions, so that what the producers gain in time they lose in quantity—that is to say, although their returns come to them quicker, yet they are compelled to get a smaller profit upon each return as a compensation for the uncertainty to which the warehouseman becomes exposed by the fluctuations in the retail market consequent upon fashion and new productions.

It is of great importance to the country at large, and to producers and labourers in particular, that there should be some certainty in the employment of labour and capital, and in cases where the tendency to over-production and change of fashion is great, there is a corresponding tendency to periodic fits of over-exertion and idleness, times when there is a great alternation between the production and consumption of capital; and these alternating seasons, although good in moderation, yet may possibly become killing to trade by their intensity, the power of recovery being lost. Moreover, this fluctuation is productive of a gambling tendency, and a desire to get up corners in a market of a particular sort, causing trade exchanges to resemble stock exchanges, and doing really a great deal more subjective harm than objective good.

6. *Fallacies respecting taxation.*—The perusal of the section of Mr. J. S. Mill's "Political Economy," headed as above, has suggested some thoughts upon his remarks, which conclude with telling his opponents " that their error is in not looking directly at the realities of phenomena, but attending only to the outward mechanism of paying and spending," which being interpreted, means that the vulgar mind will persist in considering matters subjectively and not objectively, as Mill would like them to do.

The question Mill seems to be discussing is, Does

an income tax levied on the upper and middle classes of society ultimately fall on the lower?

Every tax subjectively regarded may be divided into two portions. It takes away a portion of a man's savings and also a portion of his spendings. If AB has an income of £100 per annum and he would spend on an average £90 and save £10, and he is taxed say £10, then we think he would probably spend £85 and save £5, at any rate let us so regard it for the moment.

To the extent of his reduced productive consumption the producers are directly injured. He will consume £5 worth less of commodities per annum, therefore £5 worth less need be produced, so that both rich and poor are equally injured.

To the extent of his reduced reproductive consumption he is injured directly, but the injury to the poor may or may not take place if the £5 would have been employed in reducing the labour employed in the production of any existing commodity. So far they are benefited, but if it would have been employed in producing something fresh, they are injured by its abstraction, so that the question of benefit or injury, and who gets most of it, becomes a very complicated question.

As regards the productively consumed £5, the poor are injured. As regards the other, or reproductive consumption, a benefit has been conferred in the most usual case by prevention of injury, but the benefit is not so great as the injury, for the labour which the productive consumption would give was greater than that which the reproductive consumption would abstract, but the reproductive consumption might have been productive of increased labour greater than that abstracted by the productively consumed £5, so that the sum might come to the addition of two injuries. So that the ultimate probability is that the poor are injured a trifle more than the rich, the injury to the latter being directly subjective, that is to say, they get less to consume.

But another view must be looked at. What does the Government do with the money? Surely employ labour, so that they are merely compelling a given form of spending on the rich. They turn the consumption into other channels and so increase it. Therefore the ultimate result is that the poor don't suffer at all, for what in the first case is taken from them is in the second given back to them, and the rich alone are injured in being forced to restrict their consumption.

Perhaps the most interesting sentence in this section in Mill's book is the following: "No one is benefited by mere consumption except the person who consumes." It explains so fully and thoroughly objective economy, its aims and objects. Taking cotton stockings as an instance and looking at the above dictum, you see that he who wears cotton stockings wears what no man laboured to produce—they grow spontaneously on man's feet. To suppose a producer would be to suppose a benefit conferred on some one else other than the wearer of cotton stockings, which is utterly erroneous.

The ingenious argument by means of which this astounding dictum is arrived at is as follows :—

Capital employs labour ; capital is things employed in production ; things merely consumed are not capital, *ergo*, they do not employ labour, and therefore, lastly but not leastly, they are produced without labour, *i.e.*, spontaneously.

It is perhaps, too, a little startling to know that a weaving machine is capital. That capital employs labour, and therefore that the weaving machine employs men. Such are some of the wonders of objective argument.

7. *Of the capital of the country.*—We have seen how capital is produced, particularly or by the individual, and it seems that, therefore, inasmuch as our particulars and generalities agree, some means should be at hand by which we can judge the value and extent of the capital of the country.

Capital when employed becomes fixed.

In the primitive case supposed man hoards up a stock greater than will supply his necessary consumption for a given time. He fixed on a certain quantity, and he calls that his effective demand. This quantity exchange settles for us, and that which remains over and above the effective demand we call capital. It is evident that this excess may be utilized in employing labour upon something else, and that something else will take a more fixed and permanent form, because it will not be productively consumed.

The general state of the civilization being similar to that of the primitive state, although not of course the same, the amount of excess which remains over at the end of a year's exchanges will be the capital of the country with which it may employ reproductive labour.

The productions of some reproductive labour are naturally more fixed, that is, are not so quickly consumed as some others, and upon the fixity of the form will to a certain extent depend the amount of the capital of the country at any one time; but it will be noted that the more fixed capital becomes the less labour must be employed about it. A reservoir of water will last for generations without any great quantity of labour being employed upon it, whereas a railway by its nature gets perpetually worn out and replaced.

According then as you regard the country as a land or a people, so will your ideas be of the benefit or injury conferred by the fixity of form which the investment of capital takes. Subjectively, fixity of the form of investment of capital is an injury; objectively, it is a benefit.

All these forms of investment are objectively the capital of the country. They are the result of previously accumulated excesses of supply. The country forms a sort of reservoir into which the excess of every year is being poured through a medium of labour.

The expansion of this reservoir is therefore of the very highest importance to the country, but at the same time, as in most cases, that expansive power is limited, and great difficulty is experienced in consequence of finding new modes for the employment of capital which are not illusory and are capable of still yielding a continued return for the outlay. To this want of expansion may in a great measure be traced the recuperative powers of a country after any calamity. The destruction of the reservoir which the excess leads to is reconstruction upon a larger footing. The tramway which served very well before is turned into a railway, and in many other ways business starts on a larger footing, and, as a consequence, larger capital is caused by greater inequality in exchange. The buying power of any commodity is raised in respect of any other commodity by the restriction of the former, and therefore the effective demand represented by the latter rises.

The question then of whether the production of

See Errata on back page

capital is excessive or not, depends upon the extent of the capability of its reproductive employment, and that depends almost entirely upon our finding new methods of creating an effective demand. If a new railway, road, or canal, or a mine is opened, there is capital reproductively employed in opening it, but whether or no a benefit has been conferred or the capital has been wasted depends upon the effective demand for coals. If people cease to burn coals then the capital is wasted, so that the reproductive employment of capital is always a speculation, though the speculative character of its employment depends upon the newness of the product, the more entirely new the form of expenditure the greater speculation it becomes. When the Darlington railway was opened it was doubtful whether the money spent upon it was not (so far as a return was looked for) thrown away. But the building of a new railway now can generally be estimated as a remunerative investment for capital or not pretty accurately, though the amount of the remuneration will vary considerably, in consequent of other things than density of population.

8. *Effects of defraying Government expenditure by loans.*—This question has been pretty fully discussed by Mr. J. S. Mill, Book I, chap. v, sec. 8, from the objective point of view. Having deduced from his

preceding propositions that capital employs labour, and having started the supposition that the Government loans are defrayed from capital, it follows that as they cannot come from fixed capital they must come from circulating capital, and so are simply the result of the impoverishment of the working classes during the period of the borrowing, and having starved the working classes for a time to pay the loan, as their labour still continues to produce as much as before, it follows that all the benefit of the injury done to the poor goes to the rich. Now the facts admitted by Mr. J. S. Mill of the prosperity which was apparently caused by the Continental wars at the beginning of the century completely upset this argument, for the great apparent prosperity of that time was the prosperity of the poor as well as the rich.

Moreover, there is a slight hiatus in Mill's argument, which is, that the poor, according to him, continue to labour ~~result~~, notwithstanding the abstraction of vast quantities of circulating capital which is the means of employing them.

Very little more needs be said concerning the objective view, it remains to consider the matter subjectively. To do so we must suppose the country divided into producers and consumers. According to the theory of consumption, it will be seen at once that the primary injury falls on consumers. The

Government in obtaining a loan are merely obtaining the means of paying for a certain quantity of things which they have productively consumed. It is necessary that these things should be produced before the Government can use them, and the consequence is that producers have, as it were, to produce a greater quantity of commodities than before. This is tantamount to a restricted production so far as the ordinary consumers are concerned, for the strain put upon production cannot be momentarily responded to without affecting the previous production, so that a quantity of labour and capital is displaced, as it were, to produce for the Government. The result of any such restricted production, so far as the ordinary consumers are concerned, is that they must pay a higher price for what they consume, they must, therefore, do one of three things. They must work harder to produce the commodities to pay for the things they buy, or they must consume some of their previously accumulated capital, or they must restrict their productive consumption. Now, which ever of these things they do, except the last one, they benefit the country. If they save in order to make both ends meet, the country is directly injured, for a class are giving up labour and progress for ease and stagnation. If they produce more, then even the objectivists will admit the good; if they consume, as they generally do, from capital, the working classes are benefited for the quantity of labour employed in proportion to the capital is increased, and a stimulus is at the same time given to the producers to accumulate their capital.

It will be seen, then, that subjectively we may consider the raising of a loan by the Government as a great stimulus to trade, it is productive of a vast increase in production, and at the same time of a vast increase in the capital of the country, for there is an apparent restriction of production so far as ordinary consumers are concerned.

The three methods of payment resorted to by consumers will all be put in motion at once, and not merely one at a time, but one will naturally predominate more than the others, and upon which form the payment takes will the benefit or injury rest.

Now, however much objective economy may tell us that powder and shot, men's jackets, and boots grow spontaneously, common sense tells us that labour is employed in producing them, and also that they are paid for with the produce of other labour; so that the Government which requires these commodities is really employing not merely the labour which produces them, but some other labour, the labour which pays for them; the Government itself does not labour in producing objects or commodities to pay for them, but some one must, and that some one is the consumer; this injury, if it be an injury, of being compelled to labour at production for a reward, falls upon the consumer simply and no one else.

But while the injury, or, we prefer to call it, the benefit, falls on the consumer is reduced by being spread, that which falls to the producer is increased by concentration. Every man, woman, and child in the country is a consumer, and so they are all affected, whereas only a portion of the population are engaged in production, so that whereas the increased labour which is considered such a hardship is put upon the whole population, the labour of the producers is lightened in proportion to the consumption of the ordinary consumers, while it is increased really by having a fresh supply of customers, the Government.

But it becomes necessary to add a few words concerning capital—that is, the capital of fixed form. It will be evident that any Government loan must reduce the value of this to a certain extent, and that extent will depend upon the method of payment adopted by consumers; such fall in value taking place according to the quantity of the capital transferred to Government, every such transfer reducing the value of the capital invested elsewhere. This fall in value will, however, not be permanent, for the increasing amount of capital resulting from the productive expenditure of the Government will very soon bring up the value to what it was originally.

9. *Is it better to raise the whole of the supplies within the year?*—Objective theory has decided this question in the affirmative; practice and subjective theory naturally gives an answer in the negative.

Both Mill and Chalmers are in favour of raising the whole sum required in the year—that is, in those cases where the country lends the money to its own Government; in other cases—that is, where the loans are supplied from other countries, Mill prefers the usual system of borrowing.

Upon the supposition that the Government borrows at home—that is to say, in those cases where the things consumed are home productions, it is beneficial to obtain the money by loans, for not only is trade stimulated thereby at the time in consequence of the loan, but a great increase taking place in the forms of fixed investment which are open to those who save, and the means of future consumption are thereby vastly increased. The sums which are obtained through taxation to pay the interest are obtained from the public at large, and go into the hands of a few, thereby increasing the total power of consumption, so ultimately benefit the many.

In those cases, however, in which the supplies are raised within the year, the effect of taxation would be so heavy as to be injurious to the country, moderation in taxation being beneficial, as it is in most other things.

Naturally there is nothing more damaging to any country than its raising its loans abroad instead of at home, for not only is stimulus to labour given out of the country, as the loan is not money but goods, but it puts the borrowing nation in the hands of the lending one, for they are enabled not merely to say in what form of goods they prefer to be repaid, but also they are arbiters of the value of the goods which are to be paid, and if the state of trade is such that almost all the things which the lending country desires to consume, not only can be but are produced within it, then the borrowers are compelled either to go bankrupt or produce cheaper than the lender, in which case the value of their goods falls in proportion to their compulsory abundance, so that the depressing effects of the loan fall with ever-increasing power.

Chalmers, like Mill, thinks the labourers in effect really pay the money to the Government, that the loan is taken from circulating capital; but this is seeing only one half of the question, for it is supposing that the wages of labour can be permanently affected by Government, a most erroneous supposition.

If we consider the matter purely objectively, abolishing from our minds all idea of capital, it becomes clear that more goods must be produced within the time when the Government require those goods, but the number of labourers is not to any great extent increased, therefore their wages must rise; for commodities pay for commodities, and more commodities in the aggregate, and the same amount of labour means more for the labourer. It is true that by introducing into this view capital, some of the wages of labour are deducted in the form of interest for capital, but to suppose that labourers are so completely at the mercy of the capitalists that the latter suck all the benefit, is merely to suppose an increase of labour in excess of the amount required, which excess cannot arise in so short a period. Put the case concretely, and perhaps the view will be simpler; suppose the annual consumption of nails to be represented by 100, and that ten labourers are employed in producing them, and suppose by reason of the declaration of war the Government require ten nails more, then we should say that unless the number of labourers is augmented by one, the labourers must be benefited, for ten men are now required to produce more which they would fail to do without extra payment. If of the original 100 nails 50 go in payment of the labour and 50 in return for the capital invested, then on the increased production the wages of labour would be 55 and the return of capital 55. To suppose labour such a powerless factor in production that the greater the amount produced the smaller become the wages seems a false supposition, except when you take such long periods of time as will enable the labourers to increase and multiply beyond the proportionate increase in the amount produced. The wages of labour fall, over a series of years, because the labourers multiply faster than the production and consumption, in a word because of the innate tendency to save. Every man who spends either labours himself, or gets some one else to perform the labour for him, if he has got capital by previous over-exertion or production in excess of consumption, then he can employ labour without labouring himself, but if he has no capital, he must labour to produce something himself.

These views are of course the very reverse of those expressed by objectivists, whose idea of the height of bliss and economy may be said to be the possession and acquisition of all things in idleness, and the reasons given by Mill in the note to the section dealing with this point are precisely the reverse of those here expressed. The evil from which France suffers both now (according to one of their leading statesmen) and during the Napoleonic wars, was lack of consumption; all the things consumed were produced, as Mill says, by foreigners, and the wages rose in France not from an increase of consumption, but from a diminution of the number of the working population below the number formerly required to produce the things consumed.

France, and France alone suffered by those exhausting wars, whereas the conquered countries positively benefited. The great motor power in subjective economy is consumption, and he who consumes most produces most, and therefore proves the exertion of the greatest quantity of productive labour.

10. *Do wages come from capital?*—This question, in common with many other even oxthodox economists, we answer chiefly in the negative. The wages of those persons who are employed in producing things which are not directly called commodities, do undoubtedly come out of capital; whereas the wages of those who produce things which are directly called commodities come not from those commodities which they produce, but from some other commodities which are produced contemporaneously.

The man who is employed to-day in making stockings is paid theoretically from the other produce of to-day, but the man who is employed in making steam engines is paid from the surplus production of yesterday.

If we trace the production of capital back to its simplest form as explained in the preceding sections, we see that man first satisfies to-day's wants from to-day's labour, and having got a surplus over he can either himself labour in producing something which he does not immediately desire to consume, or he can with the surplus from to-day pay some one else to labour to-morrow. In the first case the wages and the production are simultaneous, and in the second case they are successive.

It need hardly be pointed out that the amount of productive labour is vastly in excess of reproductive labour, and therefore that most wages are simultaneous. Every man employs by consumption simultaneous labour, whereas very few employ successive labour.

The errors of economists on this point seem to be due to the very fault which they are so fond of charging their opponents with, first, regarding money as capital, and second, rushing into complex phenomena before they have studied simple cases.

The wages which are paid to the weavers and spinners can only be said to come out of capital by regarding money as capital, but what the labourer really gets is the things he buys with the money. He is really paid in beef, clothing, and cabbages, productions simultaneous with his; but it will be retorted, the case is the same with the mechanic employed on a steam engine, but this is not so, for if there had been no excessive production yesterday it would be impossible without starvation to build an engine to-day. Man must live, and steam engines are very far from being edible, and had we nothing over at the end of the day in edibles, we should be compelled to produce more edibles to-morrow or starve.

BOOK IV.

The Objectively Subjective View of Wealth —Exchange.

I. *Preliminary remarks upon exchange.*—There is no part of the science of Political Economy which requires such a comprehensive knowledge of the subject as exchange. Those things to which we attach the word wealth—as when we say coin is wealth—have the word wealth attached to them because they are exchangeable. If coin ceased to be exchangeable no one would think of calling it wealth, though the word might be applied to a person because he possessed it—the coin.

Things which are exchangeable have an altruistic value. Any thing may have a value, but it does not follow that it can be exchanged, but every thing which can be exchanged must have a value to some one other than its possessor.

Whereas in our chapter on value we were called upon to consider the development of one into all—that is to say, to show how value originating from the one and individual mind was ultimately transferred to other minds, and so into matter; now we have to consider the all-resolved into one, and that one the other. To proceed upon what Hegel calls the process of Heterization. Taking the exchange of a hat for a sovereign as an instance, it is necessary to its proper consideration that you view the matter from a light different to and other than that of the parties of the exchange. You must put yourself outside, as it were, what you are considering, if you wish to get a comprehensive view of the matter. It seems to us that this is just where economists fail in treating of exchange. They persist in regarding the matter egoistically, or from the interior view of the transaction. They tell us for instance that the hat and the sovereign perform equal services to the parties exchanging, and that therefore they exchange; now if we do what every practical man does, that is, put ourselves outside the transaction and ask the question—Do the hat and the sovereign perform equal services to parties other than those who exchange them?—we see at once the inequality, an inequality so patent that no one can deny it.

We cannot help again quoting from Hegel.

" The idea, however, demonstrates itself as thought directly identical with itself, and this at the same time as the power to set itself over against itself in order to be for itself, and in this other only to be by itself." This seems precisely to express what we do in thought concerning exchange. We consider the exchange of hat and sovereign and then we set our thoughts over against themselves, and so deny what at first sight seemed obvious. We limit the equality by inequality; we say the thing is perhaps egoistically true, yet for that reason it must be altruistically false, and it is upon this otherness of view that the truth rests. Simple though the act, consciously as we do it, yet words are almost powerless to express the action of one mind consciously to the other.

It is of course possible to view the matter altruistically from the individual view, and in this case the inequality in exchange is still apparent. Ask the hatter whether what he gets the other thing in exchange, the sovereign is equal in its value to him to the hat, and he will answer no, or I should not have sold the hat. I sold it because I got more than I gave, and so far as the other man, the purchaser, is concerned, his effective demand was equal to the supply, and there is no reason for supposing the value of the sovereign was less to him than the hat, though it certainly was not worth more. Put yourself in the purchaser's shoes, and the result is the same. He would reason as follows:—The fact that I gave a sovereign and got a hat proves the equality of my demand for hats and the supply of them; whereas I know the hatter got a profit or he would not have sold me the hat, and therefore there must have been inequality in exchange in any other than the egoistic or universal view.

It is a most curious fact therefore, that economists of the Mill school just reverse the whole process of economy. They treat production altruistically, that is, objectively, and then, in consequence, they turn round and view exchange egoistically, and so subjectively, and argue about under supplies of money as being the cause of commercial crisis, the truth being, of course, just the reverse, and commercial crisis arising when money is the cause, from an over supply of money in the producer's hands and a consequent depreciation in price or value. They take cause for effect and effect for cause, and deny abstractedly what is concretely obvious.

Never in the whole range of human thought has so much error come from not having clear and distinct ideas, from scoffing at metaphysical niceties of definition, and considering we can explain abstractedly ideas which we do not understand concretely. It is hardly either to be supposed that economists will abandon their crude abstractions for the truer, because concrete knowledge of the practical man, and will cease to tell us that prejudice is the fountain of mercantile jargon, and mercantile jargon the crystallizer of prejudice.

It is hardly necessary here to argue the question of the equality of intrinsic value in exchange. The exchange of a hat and a sovereign proves inequality in the intrinsic value of two things which exchange, so that view the matter how we may it can only be asserted that inequality is the parent of exchange, and equality is the cause of its death. When benefit ceases to accrue, when we cease to get more than we give, we shall cease to exchange one thing for another.

2. *Of money, the medium of exchange theoretically considered.*—Ideas about money seem to fluctuate in the same manner as ideas about economy, from the subjective to the objective view and *vice versâ*. From the macute, the money of idea, to the sovereign, the type of materiality. The macute is simply an idea. "There is no real thing called a macute," says Mr. J. S. Mill, at Book III, chap. vii, sec. 1, and this suffices to show us that money is an abstract idea. We have explained that wealth originally means the sensation of satisfaction produced by a material object, and it therefore follows naturally that anything which is to act as the medium or measure of exchange should enable us to measure our satisfactions.

In order to do this it is not necessary that money should be materially expressed, far less that its extrinsic and intrinsic value should coincide, as in the case of a sovereign; our satisfactions cannot be in many cases expressed materially, and so an idea such as the macute answers very well. Nothing illustrates this truth so well as the fact that we call a sovereign indifferently a sovereign and a pound. When we talk of pounds we use the word abstractedly to express our idea, by which we measure our mind just in the same way as the savages when they say a thing is worth 10 or 20 macutes. But when we use the word sovereign, we mean a positive concrete object which bears upon it marks showing that it is used to express the abstract idea pound a pound. The expression so much cavilled at by economists, that the stamp gives money, that is coin, its value conveys the idea above expressed, and means gives to money or coin the power of measuring egoistic value, that is our individual satisfactions. The mere intrinsic value is no measure of egoistic value. I, the individual, may or may not value a lump of gold, and so far the sovereign gets its value originally from the stamp, that is to say, from the idea, but in order to measure altruistic value it is essential that the idea of money should be materially expressed, that it should be conveyed into an object, and the sovereign becomes *par excellence* the best coin in the world for not only has it power to measure subjective altruistic value, but it has also from its intrinsic value the power to measure objective value.

The extremely objective tendency of the human mind has rendered the words shillings and pence almost entirely concrete. It is more impossible to sever in the mental consideration of shillings the object and the idea, partly, no doubt, because one does not require to use the ideas in the same abstract way. It is somewhat doubtful also, whether one could mentally conceive a measure proceeding by subdivision instead of multiplication, and we should say that it was impossible from the naturally synthetic tendency of mind.

It is not essential that coin should be made of gold or silver, as economists have fully pointed out. Many other material objects have been used as money, and the difference between barter and the use of other objects for money, consists in the mental idea under which they are used and which is expressed in them.

Money is a measure, and like every other known measure it is an abstract idea materially expressed. A measure means primarily a limit, and a measure of wealth or value is therefore caused by putting a limit to our desires or to the things we desire. If any thing takes our fancy, that is, when we desire it, we generally say we would give so much, thereby putting a limit on to something to express the limit and extent of our desire, and money is that by means of which this limit is usually expressed. It may be expressed upon paper or on coin, but the limit which makes it a measure is not necessarily to be expressed upon one thing any more than another, and as is shown by the macute, need not be materially expressed at all. It is not, however, to be supposed that the utilization of the measure, as a measure, will enable us to exchange one thing for another; because I say a thing is worth to me a pound, it does not follow that I have a sovereign to give for it, or the objective value of a sovereign, which is essential, if it is to be made use of as a measure of altruistic value, or the value of the thing to some one else other than the person who values.

So much for the theory of money as a medium of exchange. It shows us that money does not require material value, so far as it is a measure; neither does it require material value, so far as it is a measure of egoistic value, but that as respects its use in measuring altruistic values in exchange, it must be backed up by material value. Though it is not necessary that the material value should coincide with the measure, as in the case of a sovereign—for a cheque is money—it has the primary attributes of money, but its secondary quality or its material value can only be obtained at the bank upon which it is drawn.

While on this subject of money, theoretically considered, it will be as well just to notice the arguments which economists make use of to show that bank notes are money. Mill writes:—" The reason given for considering bank notes as money is, that by law and usage they have the property in common with metallic money of finally closing the transactions in which they are employed, which no other mode of paying one debt by transferring another has that privilege." This argument shows that bank notes are rendered by the Legislature in all cases but one equivalent to coin, and in that bank notes are the transition stage from cheques, the money of mind, to coin, the money of matter; they are in effect coin, though not in reality so.

It seems intensely hard to make people see that money is a measure, and that the idea of making intrinsic value the essence of a measure is absurd, *qua* the measure. It would be as reasonable to say that the essence of a yard is cane because shopkeepers measure with a cane yard. But money has to measure intrinsic value, and to do that it must have intrinsic value, either actually or by supposition. If money be a measure, then intrinsic value is not a primary or essential quality of it.

Money is the name given to the standard measure

of desire, just as a yard is the standard measure of length, and that intrinsic value has nothing to do with one measure originally any more than another. Though, in consequence of what it is required to measure, intrinsic value becomes ultimately necessary if the measure is to be a good and universal one. Economists' ideas about coin and money are too mixed at present. They make the words synonymous when they are essentially different. Bank notes and cheques are money, but the Legislature has made the former in effect coin which the latter certainly are not.

3. *Of money, or the medium of exchange practically considered.*—The above considerations help us very materially in forming some conclusions concerning what are technically termed commercial crises, and enable us at once to see why it is that at a crisis it becomes not only useful but necessary to lower the bullion reserves at the Bank of England. Objective economists have naturally considered that a crisis is caused by an under supply of money, and that consequently in a crisis it is the business of the Bank of England to try and increase its stock of objective money or bullion so as to enable more purchases to be made; not only, however, is this theory denied by facts, but as Professor Price points out in his " Practical Political Economy," p. 461, " the lowering of the Bank reserves at the crisis of 1866 was

carried out amidst the vehement applause of the most ardent preachers of salvation by gold."

Brisk trade is caused by great inequality in exchange, sellers get large profits on their transactions, and the competition of individuals for these large profits very soon reduces them. In proportion as these profits are reduced, exchange draws nearer and nearer to equality, and in a crisis the tendency is for the inequality to step over the boundary line, sellers are compelled to sell, and consequently, instead of getting more than they give, or a profit, they get less, or a loss.

In so far as there is perfect equality of exchange, objective money is useless, for payment is made by cheques or bills which are backed by goods. Barter is really taking place, and money in the shape of cheques is merely the measure which proves the equality.

Bullion or objective money is used to pay for the balance of goods over and above the equality, when that balance is in favour of sellers or producers. In times of brisk trade the Bank of England hold their reserve on behalf of producers, and to a certain extent it represents the amount paid by consumers to producers in excess of the equality of exchange. As profits diminish, the reserve naturally falls; for the excess of supply, for which payment has to be made in bullion by consumers, is getting reduced by competition.

The bullion may then be described as floating over into the public pockets, into the pockets of the small consumers, and consequently in a great measure tend to raise prices, and helps to restore the balance of trade in favour of producers.

Producers deal in goods and not in bullion, and consequently when the markets are unfavourable to them, bullion in the coffers of the Bank of England is useless; it does not enable the public to buy more or to raise their prices, for they have probably got quite as much as they want, and would not buy more in proportion to a reduced price, which is essential if producers are to get a profit.

We do not mean for a moment to assert that the bullion at the Bank of England represents the totality of excess or supply, but merely that it is the head or culminating point, that the Bank is the type of commercial society at the time.

Professor Price has taken a great deal of trouble to explain to his readers that the raising of the Bank rate is not dependent upon the bullion reserves, that considerations unknown to the commercial world and known to the directors of the Bank are the operative cause of a rise in the Bank rate.

Those who consider the above explanation of the matter, will see that in times of steady and fair trade a rise in the Bank rate should follow upon the lowering of the reserve, but that with an exterior declining market no rise would take place notwithstanding a decrease in the reserves; and that, therefore, when we see in City articles a notice of a diminishing reserve and the assumption that the rate will rise, the wish for good trade has been father to the thought, that the Bank directors will proclaim to the world that it is so. The action of the Bank directors follows upon and does not control the market, and the Bank rate must rise in proportion to the excess of supply, or the increase in the profit on trading transactions, for it is this which the Bank reserves have to represent or materially express.

4. *Of profit objectively considered.*—One of the objects of this book is to show why theory and practice in Political Economy are at variance, and that is the reason with which we have introduced this section. We hope to show that inasmuch as Political Economists of the Mill type persist in arguing objectively, and because every commercial man argues subjectively, therefore because subject and object are opposed, theory and practice disagree.

In order to argue objectively, you must beg the question subjectively—that is, you must assume an eternity of desire in man, that is to say, an unlimited desire—a desire which no amount of production will satisfy; and moreover it results that every question of exchange which the public consider altruistically the objectivists must regard egoistically; and no better instance of this can be produced than the following, culled from Mr. J. S. Mill. We extract the passage at full length, beginning with Mill's common assumption that subjectivists see only half of the question, or, as he calls it this time, the outside of the matter, which means that he will argue the altruistic question of profit, the result of exchange, from the egoistic or universal view (see Book II, chapter xv, sec. 6) :—

"To popular apprehension it seems as if the profits of business depended upon prices. A producer or dealer seems to obtain his profits by selling his commodity for more than it cost him. Profit altogether, people are apt to think, is a consequence of purchase and sale. It is only (they suppose) because there are purchasers for a commodity that the producer of it is able to make any profit. Demand, customers, a market for the commodity, are the cause of the gains of capitalists. It is by the sale of their goods that they replace their capital and add to its amount.

"This, however, is looking only at the outside surface of the economical machinery of society. In no case we find is mere money, which passes from one person to another, the fundamental matter in any economical phenomenon. If we look more narrowly into the operations of the produce we shall perceive that the money he obtains for his commodity is not the cause of his having a profit, but only the mode in which his profit is paid to him.

"The cause of profit is, that labour produces more than is required for its support. The reason why agricultural capital yields a profit is because human beings can grow more food than is necessary to feed them while it is being grown, including the time occupied in constructing the tools and making all other needful preparations, from which it is a consequence that if a capitalist undertakes to feed the labourers on condition of receiving the produce, he has some of it remaining for himself after replacing his advances. To vary the form of the theorem, the reason why capital yields a profit is because food, clothing, materials, and tools last longer than the time which was required to produce them, so that if a capitalist supplies a party of labourers with these things on condition of receiving all they produce, they will, in addition to reproducing all their own necessaries and instruments, have a portion of their time remaining to work for the capitalist. We thus see that profit arises not from the incidence of exchange, but from the productive power of labour, and the general profit of the country is always what the productive power of the country makes it, whether any exchange takes place or not."

This passage requires careful consideration from

the reader, because he is told he only sees the outside surface of the matter.

Mr. Mill tells us that the cause of agricultural profit is that human beings grow more food than is necessary for their sustenance and support, while it is being grown. Therefore, we conclude, agricultural profit is excess of supply, but Mr. Mill tells us this is irrational and absurd. Then we are requested to divide producers into capitalists and labourers, and so the excess is deposited into the hands of the capitalists. Then again, as excess of supply is absurd, it becomes necessary that the capitalists should consume it all; but capital is saved, that is, the capitalist forbears to consume it, so he magnanimously gives it to labourers as wages, who keep on producing fresh excesses of supply, which he continues to consume either productively or reproductively, and so on eternally. No man's wants are ever satisfied, and so production goes on without any benefit to man. All this, as will be seen, begs the question subjectively. In the first place the capitalist having got hold of the excess of supply, may either consume it in idleness or spend it reproductively, but his desires for productive or reproductive consumption are not unlimited, and a time must come, however irrational and absurd it may be, when he will cease to the latter and will consume in idleness, and then the ill effects of capital will vent themselves on the labourer. So much for the view of the profits which accrue to the noble savage who does not exchange his goods from the objective egoistic view; but let us turn the matter round and look at it subjectively or altruistically, or in the light of common sense.

A producer who exchanges his agricultural profits gets his profit from the exchange; he gives his quarters of corn for wine, we will suppose, and so the excess of supply or profit arises not in the form of corn, but in the form of wine. He estimates by money the average outside public desire for that wine, and then he refuses to part with his corn till the amount of the desire of the purchaser for his corn is in excess of the amount of the public desire for the wine he is getting, by which means the value of what he gets is greater than the value of what he gives altruistically; consequently the excess arises not in the things sold or produced, but in the things with which they are bought.

As a matter of fact, the whole transactions take place by means of money, and the desires in the question are gauged thereby, and the excess although balanced by bullion is ultimately transferred into some material object.

The idea of putting profit under the head of distribution seems to point to an utterly unpractical and erroneous method of dealing with the subject; an endeavour to regard the matter from the view of property, that is objectively instead of subjectively from the operation of exchange.

5. *Of the value of money as the indicator of its reproductive employment.*—From what we have said concerning exchange and the bank rate, it follows that the higher the rate rises or the greater the excess of supply, the larger must be the quantity of capital which it is desired to employ reproductively.

So that the amount of bullion at the bank not only indicates the state of trade, whether prosperous or otherwise, but it also indicates the spirit of progress.

There are two forms of material desire, the productive and the reproductive, and capital accrues, that is, becomes fixed in form, as desire is drawn from the productive to the reproductive form.

If it be desired to build a great railway or to make a canal, a quantity of capital must be spent to do it. In order then to get capital, sellers must demand higher prices; or to look at the matter objectively, the vendors of corn for instance transfer a large portion of the yearly supply to reproductive employment. This limits the supply for directly productive consumption, and those who directly consume must pay higher prices or give more to get that which they desire to consume, and so a greater excess arises. In consequence of this excess it follows that the Bank of England will raise the rate of discount, so as to cause an increased supply of bullion to pay for the excess, therefore the bank rate will indicate the amount of reproductive employment, as well as an increase of productive employment, for men will soon set labour to work to reduce the extra profits of the productive employer of labour.

The error therefore of all objective argument is, that it assumes an unlimited demand for the employment of capital, a state of things never existent. No human demand is unlimited of whatever nature it may be, and although the fact that we cease to consume productively, will enable us if we so desire to consume reproductively, yet it does not follow, as economists erroneously suppose, that we shall do so, and unless we do so what is saved is wasted, and what is spent is gained.

The amount of unemployed capital in the country is sufficient, one would have thought, to have proved to any person the absurdity of Mill's famous argument concerning excess of supply. Unemployed capital is commodities incapable of being profitably employed, represented by money. It is objective wealth wasting itself because subjective wealth is absent. It is commodities which will not exchange because there is no possibility of causing an excess of supply by exchange; the wants of the owners of the different sorts being equally present or absent, for either will prevent exchange.

While then the bank rate of discount will indicate

the quantity of reproductive employment, it gives no insight whatever into the question of productive employment which can only be gauged by the amount of the sums which balance in the account. Taking the returns of the banker's clearing house, the sums which balance represent the labour exchanged, the amount of productive consumption, whether that labour be given in producing commodities or services is another question, a question which it would be neither easy nor profitable to settle.

The form which labour takes is not of much consequence subjectively considered. Whether I employ a man in making combs and brushes or employ a man in brushing my hair, it is all the same so far as the world is concerned and myself, also if some one else wants combs and brushes, he will employ some one else to make them. As regards the public at large, the question simply is whether people are employed, and if they get a living from their employment, so long as they do that no man has any right to stigmatize the employment as unproductive; the employer and employed both get a living and are happy, and if that end is served that is no more to wish for. And to say that the man who employs another to brush his hair instead of employing him in making combs and brushes is wasting the productive forces of the country is, to argue falsely, because objectively is to argue that useless things are better than pleasure, an argument that no sensible person would admit to be true.

6. *Of the desirability of coincidence in coin of extrinsic and intrinsic value.*—This question is one which of all others concerning money has been most thought about and argued upon. Is it good that both sorts of value should in coin be equal as is the case in a sovereign. We cannot help thinking that it is good both subjectively and objectively, that the chief monetary factor should possess both these qualities, for it then represents to the public the all of philosophy and economy. There is no view of the matter which is not represented and expressed, and the man who feels that while talking of abstract pounds he is counting concrete sovereigns, feels a stability in his measure, a power of expression which he is capable of conveying both to the savage and the civilized, to the inhabitant of his own as well as to that of another country. A sovereign is at once the macute and the current money of the merchant, the mental, the material and materio-mental measure. But while its power of measuring is thus universal, and partly on account of it, there seems an excellent reason why the division of it should not contain equal intrinsic and extrinsic value, for it is essential that money should be an immaterial measure, that it should as it were contain evidence that mind operates in the

smallest transactions of business as well as the larger, and were our shillings to contain equal values as a sovereign does, we should be making use of a dual measure which must lead to confusion; it would be like introducing a fresh yard of a different length, and no man would know which to measure by.

The sovereign is the type of unity and equality at which we all aim, and the shilling the type of the inequality by which we attain it.

The sovereign is as a coin difficult to keep in circulation, because of the coincidence of values in it, for when used among those to whom its extrinsic value is nil, its intrinsic value comes into play, and the holder is apt to melt it down and use it for other purposes.

It would be a great thing done in relation to coinage, if nations could agree to have a coin—one coin—in their circulations of the same extrinsic and intrinsic values. Subdivision might then be left to chance, for however much theory may cry up the decimal system, there is no doubt that practice prefers dividing in the method employed in this country.

The 20 mark piece of Germany coincides in extrinsic and, within a fraction, in intrinsic value with an English sovereign, and if America could be persuaded to coin a five-dollar gold coin of a similar intrinsic value, international coinage would be helped on materially, for similarity in diversity is better than identity. People do not like to loose the latter, nor is it good that they should, while similarity tends to promote commerce by facilitating it, and were Americans to start a five-dollar gold coin of the intrinsic value of a sovereign and call it a president, we cannot help thinking that it would confer a boon upon commercial circles, far outweighing any decimal system.

In commerce it is true that the actual intrinsic value of coin is but little regarded, but at the same time it is good to have a unit to start from which will measure all sorts of values. A sovereign forms merely a starting-point, and conveys from its concreteness a much better idea than a pound, though it is clear that commercial people are fonder of the expression pound sterling, which of course means the same thing as a sovereign, for sterling is but another way of expressing material—a material pound. Sterling is used to convey the idea of that which has a fixed intrinsic value, as sterling silver. A pound sterling must naturally, however, be confined to gold pounds, for a pound's intrinsic value in silver is greater than a pound's worth of silver coin,—that is, the values do not coincide.

The inequality between the values of the smaller coinage of the country seems to afford a means of payment for the depreciation in its intrinsic value through use,—that is to say, the coinage of nine-pence worth of silver into a shilling affords the mint, or might be made to afford the mint, a means of preventing the value of the shilling from going below ninepence, which its use in circulation tends to cause it to do. A greater loss, however, probably takes place upon the gold coinage, which it would be inequitable to throw on the inequality of values in silver to make up, yet it seems better both by theory and practice not to take away from the intrinsic value of a sovereign to make up the loss by the circulation of the gold.

7. *What does cost of production mean?*—But for the confusion which has arisen as the result of objective argument, the asking of this question would seem absurd. No one but an objectivist would for one moment think of putting cost of production under the head of exchange, for cost of production is an egoistically objective idea, an idea of the trouble *a* man takes to obtain *a* commodity, and is not an idea of the material expression of the trouble one man takes to obtain from another man a second form of matter,—that is to say, it has no possible concern with ratio of exchange or altruistic value. But Adam Smith and Mill have to a certain extent varied the meaning of words to suit their objective view, and so we propose to trace the steps by which this confusion is arrived at. The all of economy, that is exchange, has marvellously perverted language.

Mr. J. S. Mill then, at Book III, chap. iii, sec. 1 writes truly enough: "As a general rule, then, things tend to exchange for one another at such values as will enable each producer to be repaid the cost of production with the ordinary profit—in other words, such as will give to all producers the same rate of profit on their outlay. But in order that the profit may be equal where the outlay—that is the cost of production—is equal, things must on the average exchange for one another in the ratio of their cost of production, things of which the cost of production is the same must be of the same value." Adam Smith and Ricardo have called that value of a thing which is proportionable to its cost of production its natural value (or its natural price). The ideas, of course, are true enough things to tend to exchange for one another in the ratio of their cost of production, but they seldom do so really. What we object to is the method of stating it, and the endeavour to draw the mind away from cost of production to market value, by striving to make out that they correspond though they are not identical. This sort of desire to be objective is bound to lead to erroneous conclusions if logically followed out. It results in this case in Mill's turning cause into effect and arguing backwards, for in sec. 2 he writes: "The latent influence by which the values of things are made to conform in the long run to the cost of production is the variation that would otherwise take place in the supply of the commodity." By the word value it must be recollected Mill does not convey what the public mean by it, but in effect some other commodity, so that he really means to say that the influence by which the other commodity in exchange tends to conform in cost of production to the one in question is the variation that would take place in the supply of the latter,—that is to say, that if the cost of production of the other commodity fell it would fall, because less of the one in question must be given for it, which is putting the cart before the horse, as one would expect from his arguing objectively.

A fall in cost of production enables you to obtain the commodity in question cheaper, or with less of any other commodity, and although less of any other commodity being necessary in exchange is sometimes proof that the cost of production of the one has fallen, yet the cause does not lie, as Mill asserts, in the exchange, but in the cost of production, alteration in exchange being the effect of a lowered cost of production.

The tendency of profits to uniformity consequent upon competition for the highest, show us that cost of production must also tend to uniformity in exchange, for cost of production is the gauge by which profits are regulated. A thing costs a producer so much to make, and he tries to get as high a price as he can, while he fixes a price below which he will not go, and the profit is the result of getting more for it than its cost of production or his effective demand.

The chief element in cost of production is labour, and out of any price given for an article we think it may be fairly asserted that more than half goes directly as the reward of labour is the cost of labour. Every reduction of price therefore is proof of a reduction of labour in excess of a reduction of profit. It is so much more public starvation of the poor, though it may be balanced by a greater gain even to them, but this remains to be proved in each case.

Profit is no part of cost of production. Cost of production has no concern with exchange primarily, but it is true that exchange value, or price is the regulator of profit, and so in a measure the gauge of cost of production. Cost of production is generally considered to mean what a thing cost the man who gets the profit—before he got the profit, and not after it, as economists strive to make out.

The idea that the value of things is determined by their cost of protection is another erroneous form of objective argument. Cost of production is the evidence of egoistic value; it is evidence of the thing having a value, but it is no guide to the amount of the value which the thing represents. I may be very hungry and take some trouble to get bread, but the value of the bread measured by its cost of production may be as nil, compared to what it cost me to procure a diamond or some gold.

Again, altruistically speaking, those things which cost least to produce have very often the highest value, *e.g.*, coin and gold. The cost of production of gold is very small compared to that of coin. Compare the labour spent in producing all the gold in the world at this time and all the coin, and it will be obvious that the cost of production of that amount of the one which exchanges for the other is unequal in the highest degree.

8. *Of international trade.*—It is impossible, or it seems so to us, to understand the light in which the objectivists and Cobdenites regard money when dealing with international trade. They assert stoutly that all exchange involves equality, and that you cannot export more than you import, and they make sundry other assertions in direct contradiction of facts. It is a fact that the imports of this country exceed the exports by upwards of £200,000,000, a sufficient good inequality for all practical argument, and yet Professor B. Price writes on page 306 of his " Practical Political Economy," second edition, "We see in many quarters great pains taken in tracing out the statistics of international commerce for the purpose of showing that the country which buys of the foreigner is not

compensated by a corresponding amount of sales. This is idle and unprofitable work. It is enough to know that the trade goes on. This fact by itself alone, upon the grounds explained above (equality in exchange), demonstrates that the foreigner has bought as much as he has sold. No statistics are needed for the proof of this fact, nor if the statistics failed to point out how the equivalent has been received would the demonstration be in any way weakened. Assuredly no economist, nor indeed any thinking person, need give himself a thought, so far as this point is concerned, as to what the statistics may or may not bring out. The trade goes on; therefore selling is taking place to the same extent as buying abroad."

Now in the face of such statements as these, we are bound to confess we feel completely knocked over by their illogicality. When a man asserts theories based, as is supposed, upon facts, and finding the facts utterly at variance with the theory, denies that facts are of any concern in the matter, argument seems out of the question. However, we will try and show the arguments by which all this contradiction arises. Here is the Cobdenite argument placed in its simplest form. Wealth means commodities or material objects; money is the measure of those material objects or wealth. Consequently, speaking from the view of any particular country in trading with others, the more goods you can import and the less you can export, supposing inequality possible, the better off the country in question must be in wealth or material objects; but Professor Price adds, you cannot export more than you import, so when money is used to measure the trade in material objects between one country and another, money does not measure the material objects. We should be glad to know what it does.

Now let us take the subjective view, which will, we confess, be difficult to follow in generalities, though of the greatest possible simplicity concretely.

Wealth means satisfactions produced by material objects. That which a country can export is the excess of material objects obtained by internal exchange beyond those which are proved to be giving satisfaction by being effectively demanded.

The power of these material objects in exchange depends upon the amount of the foreigners' desire for them rising as it rises and falling as it falls, and that desire is estimated by other material objects. Those things only are exported which foreigners can be found to desire, consequently the greater the amount of the exports the greater is the desire of foreigners for our commodities, and the larger will be the quantity of the material objects which we receive in exchange for them. But the price and value of those things which are imported into this country from abroad, depends in this country upon our desire for them, rising as it rises and falling as it falls; consequently the less we import from abroad the less we are coveting other nations' goods, and the more self-sustained the nation is.

The value of the exports rising proves a greater amount of desire on the part of others for those material objects, and consequently a greater amount being received to pay for them; the value of the imports rising proves a greater desire for foreign goods, a greater inability to get on without them.

The price of exports is the measure of foreign satisfactions, the price of imports the measure of home satisfactions, and as satisfactions given to others is objective wealth to ourselves, excess of exports means excess of wealth objectively.

Objects may exchange for objects, and so there may be equality objectively, but subjectively the highest inequality not only may but does prevail.

We must confess ourselves quite at a loss to understand Professor Bonamy Price's view; how equality must be present and yet monetary inequality be proved to exist, we are quite at a loss to conceive, so long as money is regarded, whether subjectively or objectively, as a measure. No matter in what light you look at it, if money is to be in any way a measure, then inequality cannot be denied, unless the Professor supposes all trade returns to be a hoax, and got up with a view of humbugging the world.

Cobdenites should put down statistics as a hoax, so it seems, if they are logical.

Many persons of course will deny that exports are the excess of supply, so we must explain that by excess of supply is intended any commodities produced for which the producer cannot find a remunerative market at home, and which would consequently cease to be produced, though perhaps not entirely, could no foreign market be found for them.

Conclusions of the greatest importance flow from this subjective view of exchange. It has been matter of the most intense surprise to any one that a country's imports should exceed its exports by such a vast sum as £200,000,000 and upwards, and many persons have thought that bullion must go out of the country to this extent, which naturally seems an impossibility. Those of our readers who have grasped the theory of exchange will see that the statistics of exports and imports are egoistic—that is, universal statistics, and that they are in reality the gauge of two nations' desires taken together. Taken separately—that is, altruistically, or from the view of persons other than the exchangers, and it will be found that the result is more extraordinary still, for all exports are not really commodities to the exporting nation—they are valueless; they are the excess beyond effective demand, so that an exporting nation is giving that which it does not want for what it does want. Extremes, however, are said to meet, and they do so here. The first altruistic view shows us the most intense inequality, a nation giving nothing and getting something; the second view brings us nearer to equality, for the exports which to the nation are valueless would be, to a person or nation other than the traders, of a value near to that given by the foreigner, not so great of course, or they would have been exported to the other party, and similarly with the imports; to the other party their value would be greater than to the importing nation, gauged as it is by the exports, so that there may be a vast inequality apparent by statistics and yet but little in reality, and that little will be measured by bullion, the highest representative of wealth. So that one sees how nearly true and yet how far from truth is the Cobdenite idea. Cobdenites, we are afraid, will never understand that concrete knowledge is always true, generalities only sometimes, and he who contradicts what is concretely obvious to all the world, merely proclaims the partial generality of his knowledge. Particulars and generalities must be made to agree.

9. *Of the value of money.*—By the value of money is generally understood the rate of discount, the amount of discount demanded for a loan on a bill or note; but it is very clear that this is only one of

many meanings given to the idea, for economists are fond of talking of the value of money as dependent on cost of production, meaning thereby to discuss the intrinsic value of coin as dependent upon the cost of production of bullion or sterling metal.

Now, in the first case, the value of money depends almost entirely upon the amount of the reproductive forms of employment of capital. The exchange of directly satisfactory commodities in the mercantile world always tends to equality, but there are constantly springing up fresh forms of employment, fresh investments of capital, and every fresh company which absorbs capital prior to its giving a return is trenching on the equality of exchange and is causing greater inequality; it draws away a portion of produce from one class of exchangers, and then that class commonly called producers or sellers gets it back again from the other class, the consumer or buyer class, by refusing to part with the residue save upon a higher price—that is, more commodities or a greater inequality in exchange.

High value of money, then, is concurrent with good trade; it means to say that producers are struggling to satisfy a demand greater than can be satisfied all at once, and brisk times are the consequence.

With regard to the other idea of the intrinsic value of coin as dependent upon cost of production, nothing can better show the inability of economists to understand the ideas with which they deal than this method of talking about the value of coin.

Let the reader go back to what we said concerning intrinsic value, and he will see that intrinsic value has no possible concern with cost of production, but depends upon other material employment, upon our idea of the value of a thing *qua* some other thing, and consequently that the intrinsic value of bullion depends upon what is generally meant by utility, and cost of production has nothing to do with it. Gold coin, the cost of production of which is the lowest possible, has the highest intrinsic value. It is the very lowness of its cost of production that caused the rush for the Australian and Californian gold mines, every body who went expected to reap vast profit with little labour, little cost of production to themselves, and thought others slow who remained getting small profits in consequence of high cost of production. As before explained, we use the words cost of production in the vulgar sense and not in the economical sense.

Naturally it may be asked, why is the intrinsic value of gold higher than silver? and the only answer is, that people regard gold as of greater material utility; of all the purposes to which gold and silver can be turned gold is considered to have more in proportion to the supply of it than silver. Assuming the number of employments for gold and silver the same, then gold has a higher intrinsic value than silver consequent upon a more limited supply.

Another consideration of much importance may be drawn from this in considering the question of monometalism or bimetalism.

Great weight of mind has been brought to show that bimetalism is the better idea, because fluctuation in value by being spread upon two metals becomes lessened.

Stability of value is to be aimed at in a coinage, and it follows therefore from a coin being a material object that intrinsic value is the value meant, for extrinsic value is immaterial or mental. This being so, the question of how best to attain stability of value in coinage depends upon the proportion which the supply of the ingredient when made up in one form bears to the effective demands of the ingredient for use in another form. Let us take gold as an instance, and suppose the extrinsic value of the supply to be £100,000, and that £20,000 worth is annually made into jewellery and the rest into sovereigns. Now the stability of the value of the gold in the sovereigns will depend upon the proportion which the £100,000 worth, the supply, bears to the ineffective demand for the 80,000 sovereigns in another form, say gold watches, or, which is the same thing, to the effective demand for more jewellery.

Intrinsic value, then, depends upon applicability

to another purpose, and therefore monometalism must be the best form for coinage to take to prevent a depreciation of value, for by confining coinage to one metal the intrinsic value must tend to become more fixed.

If payment may be made in either one of two coined metals; the moment that the extrinsic value of one falls, payment is made directly in it, for by so doing the payer gains, but that at once lowers the intrinsic value of the other metal, and fluctuations, instead of being reduced, are positively augmented. The intrinsic value of the metal pushed out of use for a time will fall, because more will go to supply the other material demand, and that at once brings down its intrinsic value; and the reverse is also true that bimetalism increases a rise equally with the fall.

The very argument by which bimetalism is upheld seems to us therefore the weakest that could possibly be brought forward if stability of values is desired, and the endeavour to lessen fluctuation in value by, as it were, dividing the values, seems the best method of increasing it.

14, Henrietta Street, Covent Garden, London; and
20, South Frederick Street, Edinburgh.

WILLIAMS AND NORGATE'S
LIST OF
French, German, Italian, Latin, and Greek,
AND OTHER
SCHOOL BOOKS AND MAPS.

French.

FOR PUBLIC SCHOOLS WHERE LATIN IS TAUGHT.

Eugène (G.) The Student's Comparative Grammar of the French Language, with an Historical Sketch of the Formation of French. For the use of Public Schools. With Exercises. 6th Improved Edition. Square crown 8vo, cloth. 5s.

Or Grammar, 3s.; Exercises, 2s. 6d.

"The appearance of a Grammar like this is in itself a sign that great advance is being made in the teaching of modern as well as of ancient languages. . . . The rules and observations are all scientifically classified and explained. . . . Mr. Eugène's book is one that we can strongly recommend for use in the higher forms of large schools."—*Educational Times.*

"In itself this is in many ways the most satisfactory Grammar for beginners that we have as yet seen. . . . The book is likely to be useful to all who wish either to learn or to teach the French language."—*Athenæum.*

Eugène's French Method. Elementary French Lessons. Easy Rules and Exercises preparatory to the "Student's Comparative French Grammar." By the same Author. 4th Edition. Crown 8vo, cloth. 1s. 6d.

"Certainly deserves to rank among the best of our Elementary French Exercise-books."—*Educational Times.*

"To those who begin to study French, I may recommend, as the best book of the kind with which I am acquainted, '*Eugène's Elementary Lessons in French.*' It is only after having fully mastered this small manual and Exercise-book that they ought to begin the more systematic study of French."—*Dr. Breymann, Lecturer of the French Language and Literature, Owen's College, Manchester (Preface to Philological French Grammar).*

Eugène's Comparative French-English Studies, Grammatical and Idiomatic. Being a New, entirely re-written, Edition of the "French Exercises for Middle and Upper Forms." 4th Edition. Cloth. 2s. 6d.

Attwell (H.) Twenty Supplementary French Lessons, with Etymological Vocabularies. Chiefly for the use of Schools where Latin is taught. Crown 8vo, cloth. 2s.

Krueger (H.) Short French Grammar. 5th Edition. 180 pp. 12mo, cloth. 2s.

Venosta (F.) Companion to the Grammars, or List of Words, Phrases and Technical Terms in English, French, German and Italian. 454 pp. Crown 8vo, cloth. 5s.

Ahn's French Familiar Dialogues, and French-English Vocabulary for English Schools. 12mo, cloth. 2s.

Brasseur (Prof. Isid.) Grammar of the French Language, comprehending New and complete Rules on the Genders of French Nouns. 20th Edition. 12mo, cloth. 3s. 6d.

—————— **Manuel des Ecoliers.** A French Reading Book, preceded by Rules on French Pronunciation. 6th Edition. 12mo. 2s. 6d.

—————— **Premières Lectures.** An easy French Reading Book for Children and Beginners. 18mo, cloth. 1s. 6d.

Delbos (L.) French Accidence and Minor Syntax. Crown 8vo, cloth. 1s. 6d.

Strouwelle (Prof. A.) Treatise on French Genders. 12mo, cloth. 1s. 6d.

Williams (T. S.) and J. Lafont. French and Commercial Correspondence. A Collection of Modern Mercantile Letters in French and English, with their translation on opposite pages. 2nd Edition. 12mo, cloth. 4s. 6d.

For a German Version of the same Letters, vide p. 4.

Fleury's Histoire de France, racontée à la Jeunesse, edited for the use of English Pupils, with Grammatical Notes, by Auguste Beljame, Bachelier-ès-lettres de l'Université de Paris. 3rd Edition. 12mo, cloth boards. 3s. 6d.

Mandrou (A.) French Poetry for English Schools. Album Poétique de la Jeunesse. By A. Mandrou, M.A. de l'Académie de Paris. 2nd Edition. 12mo, cloth. 3s. 6d.

German.

Schlutter's German Class Book. A Course of Instruction based on Becker's System, and so arranged as to exhibit the Self-development of the Language, and its Affinities with the English. By Fr. Schlutter, Royal Military Academy, Woolwich. 4th Edition. 12mo, cloth. 5s.

—— A Key to the same. Cloth. 5s.

Möller (A.) A German Reading Book. A Companion to SCHLUTTER's German Class Book. With a complete Vocabulary. 150 pp. 12mo, cloth. 2s.

Ravensberg (A. v.) Practical Grammar of the German Language. Conversational Exercises, Dialogues and Idiomatic Expressions. 3rd Edition. Cloth. (Key, 2s.) 5s.

—— Rose's English into German. A Selection of Anecdotes, Stories, Portions of Comedies, &c., with copious Notes for Translation. By A. v. Ravensberg. 2nd Edition. Cloth. (Key, 5s.) 4s. 6d.

—— German Reader, Prose and Poetry, with copious Notes for Beginners. 2nd Edition. Crown 8vo, cloth. 3s.

—— Student's First Year's German Companion. A concise Conversational Method. 12mo, cloth. 2s. 6d.

Weisse's Complete Practical Grammar of the German Language, with Exercises in Conversations, Letters, Poems and Treatises, &c. 4th Edition, very much improved. 12mo, cloth. 6s.

—— New Conversational Exercises in German Composition, with complete Rules and Directions, with full References to his German Grammar. 2nd Edition. 12mo, cloth. (Key, 5s.) 3s. 6d.

Wittich's German Tales for Beginners, arranged in Progressive Order. 20th Edition. Crown 8vo, cloth. 6s.

—— German for Beginners. New Edition. 12mo, cloth. 5s.

—— Key to ditto. 12mo, cloth. 7s.

—— German Grammar. 7th Edition. 12mo, cloth. 6s. 6d.

Schinzel (E.) Child's First German Course; also, A Complete Treatise on German Pronunciation and Reading. Crown 8vo, cloth. 2s. 6d.

Sonnenschein and Stallybrass. German for the English. Part I. First Reading Book. Easy Poems with interlinear Translations, and illustrated by Notes and Tables, chiefly Etymological. 4th Edition. 12mo, cloth. 4s. 6d.

Eisner (J.) The German Declensions. A Practical Course, with Reading and Writing Lessons. 12mo, cloth. 5s. 6d.

Ahn's German Method by Rose. A New Edition of the genuine Book, with a Supplement consisting of Models of Conjugations, a Table of all Regular Dissonant and Irregular Verbs, Rules on the Prepositions, &c. &c. By A. V. Rose. 2 Courses in 1 vol. Cloth. 3s. 6d.

—— **German Method by Rose,** &c. First Course. Cloth. 2s.

Apel's Short and Practical German Grammar for Beginners, with copious Examples and Exercises. 2nd Edition. 12mo, cloth. 2s. 6d.

[Black's] Thieme's Complete Grammatical German Dictionary, in which are introduced the Genitives and Plurals and other Irregularities of Substantives, the Comparative Degrees of Adjectives, and the Irregularities of Verbs. Square 8vo, strongly bound. 6s.

Koehler (F.) German-English and English-German Dictionary. 2 vols. 1120 pp., treble columns, royal 8vo, in one vol., half-bound. 9s.

Williams (T. S.) Modern German and English Conversations and Elementary Phrases, the German revised and corrected by A. Kokemueller. 21st enlarged and improved Edition. 12mo, cloth. 3s. 6d.

—— **and O. Cruse. German and English Commercial Correspondence.** A Collection of Modern Mercantile Letters in German and English, with their Translation on opposite pages. 2nd Edition. 12mo, cloth. 4s. 6d.

For a French Version of the same Letters, vide p. 2.

Apel (H.) German Prose Stories for Beginners (including Lessing's Prose Fables), with an interlinear Translation in the natural order of Construction. 12mo, cloth. 2s. 6d.

—— **German Poetry.** Nearly 300 Pieces selected from 70 different Authors. Crown 8vo, cloth. 5s.

—— **German Prose.** A Collection of the best Specimens of German Prose, chiefly from Modern Authors. 500 pp. Crown 8vo, cloth. 3s.

Andersen (H. C.) Bilderbuch ohne Bilder. The German Text, with Explanatory Notes, &c., and a complete Vocabulary, for the use of Schools, by Alphons Beck. 2nd Edition. 12mo, cloth. 2s.

Chamisso's Peter Schlemihl. The German Text, with copious Explanatory Notes and a Vocabulary, by M. Förster. Crown 8vo, cloth. 2s.

Lessing's Minna von Barnhelm, the German Text, with Explanatory Notes and a Vocabulary, by J. A. F. Schmidt. 2nd Edition. 12mo, cloth. 2s. 6d.

Goethe's Hermann und Dorothea. With Notes and Vocabulary, by M. Förster. 12mo, cloth. 2s. 6d.

—— Hermann und Dorothea. With Grammatical Notes by A. von Ravensberg. Crown 8vo, cloth. 2s. 6d.

—— Egmont. The German Text, with Notes and Vocabulary, by H. Apel. 12mo, cloth. 2s. 6d.

—— Faust. With copious Notes by Falk Lebahn. 8vo, cloth. 10s. 6d.

Schiller's Maria Stuart, with copious Grammatical, Explanatory, and Historical Notes, by Moritz Förster. Crown 8vo, cloth. 2s. 6d.

Goldschmidt (H. E.) German Poetry. A Selection of the best Modern Poems, with the best English Translations on opposite pages. Crown 8vo, cloth. 5s.

Hauff's Mærchen. A Selection from Hauff's Fairy Tales. The German Text, with a Vocabulary in foot-notes. By A. Hoare, B.A. Crown 8vo, cloth. 3s. 6d.

Nieritz. Die Waise, a German Tale, with Notes and Vocabulary, by E. C. Otte. 12mo, cloth. 2s. 6d.

Carové (J. W.) Mæhrchen ohne Ende (The Story without an End). 12mo, cloth. 2s.

Schiller's Song of the Bell, German Text, with English Poetical Translation on the opposite pages, by J. Hermann Merivale, Esq. 12mo, cloth. 1s.

Fouque's Undine, Sintram, Aslauga's Ritter, die beiden Hauptleute. 4 vols. in 1. 8vo, cloth. 7s. 6d.

Undine. 1s. 6d.; cloth, 2s.   Aslauga. 1s. 6d.; cloth, 2s.
Sintram. 2s. 6d.; cloth, 3s.   Hauptleute. 1s. 6d.; cloth, 2s.

Latin and Greek.

Bryce (Rev. Dr.) The Laws of Greek Accentuation Simplified. 3rd Edition, with the most essential Rules of Quantity. 12mo, sewed. 6d.

Euripides' Medea. The Greek Text, with Introduction and Explanatory Notes for Schools, by J. H. Hogan. 8vo, cloth. 3s. 6d.

────── **Ion.** Greek Text, with Notes for Beginners, Introduction and Questions for Examination, by Dr. Charles Badham, D.D. 2nd Edition. 8vo. 3s. 6d.

Æschylus. Agamemnon. Revised Greek Text, with literal line-for-line Translation on opposite pages, by John F. Davies, B.A. 8vo, cloth. 3s.

Platonis Philebus. With Introduction and Notes by Dr. C. Badham. 2nd Edition, considerably augmented. 8vo, cloth. 4s.

────── **Euthydemus et Laches.** With Critical Notes and an Epistola critica to the Senate of the Leyden University, by Dr. Ch. Badham, D.D. 8vo, cloth. 4s.

────── **Symposium,** and Letter to the Master of Trinity, " De Platonis Legibus,"—Platonis Convivium, cum Epistola ad Thompsonum edidit Carolus Badham. 8vo, cloth. 4s.

Sophocles. Electra. The Greek Text critically revised, with the aid of MSS. newly collated and explained. By Rev. H. F. M. Blaydes, M.A., formerly Student of Christ Church, Oxford. 8vo, cloth. 6s.

────── **Philoctetes.** Edited by the same. 8vo, cloth. 6s.

────── **Trachiniæ.** Edited by the same. 8vo, cloth. 6s.

────── **Ajax.** Edited by the same. 8vo, cloth. 6s.

Kiepert's New Atlas Antiquus. Maps of the Ancient World, for Schools and Colleges. 6th Edition. With a complete Geographical Index. Folio, boards. 7s. 6d.

Kampen. 15 Maps to illustrate Cæsar's De Bello Gallico. 15 coloured Maps. 4to, cloth. 3s. 6d.

Italian.

Volpe (Cav. G.) Eton Italian Grammar, for the use of Eton College. Including Exercises and Examples. New Edition. Crown 8vo, cloth. 4s. 6d.
——— Key to the Exercises. 1s.
Rossetti. Exercises for securing Idiomatic Italian by means of Literal Translations from the English, by Maria F. Rossetti. 12mo, cloth. 3s. 6d.
——— Aneddoti Italiani. One Hundred Italian Anecdotes, selected from "Il Compagno del Passeggio." Being also a Key to Rossetti's Exercises. 12mo, cloth. 2s. 6d.
Venosta (F.) Raccolta di Poesie tratti dai piu celebri autori antichi e moderni. Crown 8vo, cloth. 5s.

Danish—Dutch.

Bojesen (Mad. Marie) The Danish Speaker. Pronunciation of the Danish Language, Vocabulary, Dialogues and Idioms for the use of Students and Travellers in Denmark and Norway. 12mo, cloth. 4s.
Rask (E.) Danish Grammar for Englishmen. With Extracts in Prose and Verse. 2nd Edition. Edited by Repp. 8vo. 5s.
Williams and Ludolph. Dutch and English Dialogues, and Elementary Phrases. 12mo. 2s. 6d.

Wall Maps.

Sydow's Wall Maps of Physical Geography for School-rooms, representing the purely physical proportions of the Globe, drawn in a bold manner. An English Edition, the Originals with English Names and Explanations. Mounted on canvas, with rollers:

1. The World. 12 Sheets. Mounted. 10s.
2. Europe. 9 Sheets. Mounted. 10s.
3. Asia. 9 Sheets. Mounted. 10s.
4. Africa. 6 Sheets. 10s.
5. America (North and South). 2 Maps, 10 Sheets. 10s.
6. Australia and Australasia. 6 Sheets. Mounted. 10s.

——— Handbook to the Series of Large Physical Maps for School Instruction, edited by J. Tilleard. 8vo. 1s.

Miscellaneous.

De Rheims (H.). Practical Lines in Geometrical Drawing, containing the Use of Mathematical Instruments and the Construction of Scales, the Elements of Practical and Descriptive Geometry, Orthographic and Horizontal Projections; Isometrical Drawing and Perspective. Illustrated with 300 Diagrams, and giving (by analogy) the solution of every Question proposed at the Competitive Examinations for the Army. 8vo, cloth. 9s.

Fuerst's Hebrew Lexicon, by Davidson. A Hebrew and Chaldee Lexicon to the Old Testament, by Dr. Julius Fuerst. 4th Edition, improved and enlarged, containing a Grammatical and Analytical Appendix. Translated by Rev. Dr. Samuel Davidson. 1600 pp., royal 8vo, cloth. 21s.

Hebrew Texts. Large type. 16mo, cloth. each 1s.
Genesis. 1s. Psalms. 1s. Job. 1s. Isaiah. 1s.

Turpie (Rev. Dr.) Manual of the Chaldee Language: containing Grammar of the Biblical Chaldee and of the Targums, and a Chrestomathy, consisting of Selections from the Targums, with a Vocabulary adapted to the Chrestomathy. 1879. Square 8vo, cloth. 7s.

Attwell (Prof. H.) Table of Aryan (Indo-European) Languages, showing their Classification and Affinities, with copious Notes; to which is added, Grimm's Law of the Interchange of Mute Consonants, with numerous Illustrations. A Wall Map for the use of Colleges and Lecture-rooms. 2nd Edition. Mounted with rollers. 10s.

—— The same Table, in 4to, with numerous Additions. Boards. 7s. 6d.

Williams and Simmonds. English Commercial Correspondence. A Collection of Modern Mercantile Letters. By T. S. Williams and P. L. Simmonds. 12mo, cloth. 4s.

Bayldon. Icelandic Grammar. An Elementary Grammar of the Old Norse or Icelandic Language. By Rev. George Bayldon. 8vo, cloth. 7s. 6d.

Levant Interpreter: a Polyglotte Dialogue Book for Travellers in the East. English, Turkish, Modern Greek and Italian. Crown 8vo, cloth. 5s.

Spencer (Herbert) Education, Intellectual, Moral and Physical. Cheap Edition. Fourth Thousand. Cloth. 2s. 6d.

www.ingramcontent.com/pod-product-compliance
Lightning Source LLC
Chambersburg PA
CBHW030303240426
43673CB00040B/1041